FACING THE
ELEPHANTS

A Woman's Journey Through Life, Death, and Finding Spiritual Connection with a Family of Elephants

REBECCA BLACK

W. Brand Publishing
NASHVILLE, TENNESSEE

W. Brand Publishing

j.brand@wbrandpub.com

www.wbrandpub.com

Cover design by JuLee Brand / designchik.net

Cover inspired by Payne Kolep

Facing the Elephants/ Rebecca Black. —1st ed.

Available in Paperback, Kindle, and eBook formats.

Paperback ISBN 978-1-950385-00-3

eBook ISBN: 978-1-950385-05-8

Library of Congress Control Number: 2019933745

CONTENTS

Original artwork by the author's son, Payne Kolep,
which inspired the final cover design.

DEDICATION

*This book is dedicated to my friends and family
who were there for me through the toughest of times.*

*To my friends Sarah and Danielle, thank you.
Russ and Roxanne, you guys have been like parents to me.*

*My amazing husband Nicolas, thank you for being loving and
supportive, and seeing my beauty no matter what.*

*To my son Sabastion for using humor to always lighten my mood
and pull out my smile.*

*And a special thank you to my son, Payne, who had an amazing
outlook on how I would make it through. He inspired the cover
of my book, he photographed me for the back of the book, and he
continues to assist me creatively in many ways.*

Thank you to all with love,

Rebecca Black

THE DAY I DIED

This is my life; lying in bed, unable to sleep. No exception tonight; I tossed and turned in my dark and a little too warm room, not unusual for an April night in Tucson. My fiancé snored, oblivious, next to me. I barely noticed the noise anymore, except when he stopped breathing for a second and then snorted like an overjoyed pig.

My small bedroom felt even smaller at night, the air stale; the air conditioning was cranked down low, but it never worked very well in my apartment. A leftover hint of vanilla hung in the air from the candles I religiously lit every night. I was known to my family for having an inhumanly good sense of smell, so I burned candles to make the air pleasant. I could barely detect the smell of fabric softener, so I knew it had been too long since the sheets were washed. *I'll wash them tomorrow after work* I mused, staring at the ceiling. This was my life . . . at this point, men had come and gone believing they were much more special than they were . . . I was trying on something new.

He still didn't fit. This was my life? Like I was a female version of Prufrock in T.S. Eliot's poem.

I could never settle my mind at night. Thoughts always wandered. As I laid there, I heard Sedona, my two-year-old dog named after the town that shares her fur's reddish hue, rustle in her kennel. She is the cutest and most bizarre mutt I have ever laid eyes on, a mind-boggling DNA verified mix of Akita and Jack Russell terrier. She had been a difficult puppy, and even now, her kennel is pulled away from the wall so she won't eat, well, the wall.

The alarm clock on my nightstand glowed red, the only light in the room. I keep the wooden shutters on the window closed to block out the dim orange lighting of the parking lot outside. Light made it even harder for me to sleep. Every night for me was long. Despite the warmth, I couldn't just sleep with a sheet—I needed blankets to provide me with a sense of security. It didn't help with getting comfortable, but I had always been that way. Everything about my nights had been normal. So far.

Abnormally, on the other hand, work that day had been good. I'd spent part of it bullshitting with my friend and co-worker, Danielle. I got my reports done. I even left on time. Weird. Work had been nothing but stress for some time. To have a decent day working at the Department of Child Services was out of the ordinary. It left me with high expectations for the next day—I was on top of my work, I would not need to go in at the crack of dawn, I could be on pace for once. I felt relieved in that sense.

After the fifteen-minute commute home from the office, another unusual thing, as many nights I came from far afield elsewhere in town, I got home and cooked dinner for my sons, the loves of my life. Spaghetti with meat sauce, one of their favorites. It was a rare pleasure those days to be able to cook for them. My hours at work usually kept me out too late to do that. Typically, I brought something home or had something steeping in the Crock Pot if my schedule foreshadowed a bad day; better known as a typical day, really. Or, if the day would be impossible, there was always frozen lasagna, usually reserved for nights I was going to get home after their bedtime. Having the chance to slow down and do something for my children always made me happy.

I sat at the dining table, a high top bistro type with four chairs; two for my boys, and the other two for me and my then fiancé, Jack. Family nights, like my chance to cook dinner, were rare, so I took it in while I could.

It being a school night, my two boys got ready for bed. Jack was lying in bed, on his phone, as he usually was when he spent the night. He was never much company; stuck behind the bluish glow of his phone screen. I decided to take advantage of my good mood, my low-stress day at work, and getting home early to try and catch up on rest. I started my nighttime routine; got in the shower, brushed my teeth, lotioned myself up and got into bed.

Nearly my entire life, I have suffered from insomnia. A holdover from my childhood where nighttime was a terrible time; where sleep was a vulnerability not worth risking. Tonight proved no different; comfort did not come easily. I laid in bed tossing, turning, wishing to be asleep, while simultaneously overanalyzing every aspect of my life. Jack lay there, a log next to me, still snoring. I figured this would be the theme for the night.

Then it happened. Pain. Awful, searing pain, rising out of nowhere like a sparked gasoline fire. It hit me like a bullet wound, bursting a hole in my right side just above my hip bone. I cried out in agony as pain radiated up into my rib cage. My body folded in half, writhing in pain. Jack continued to lie there like a log, snoring.

Ten minutes or more passed as I tried to wait out the pain. Tears flowed; I cried from the tortuous, stabbing agony.

"Uhh . . . humm . . . what's wrong?" Jack mumbled, barely conscious. In my agony, I tried and failed to explain what I was experiencing.

"I'm in awful pain," I managed to push out past it all.

Still not awake, he didn't respond, so I told him I was going to sit in a hot bath to see if that helped. I got out of bed and walked to the bathroom across the hall. My kids had the master bedroom; I made sure they always had the most space I could afford as a single mother. While making the short walk, I immediately noticed something worrisome—I couldn't stand up straight. I tried, but my body was trembling, and the pain went from agonizing to excruciating, so I held onto the walls to get across the hall to the bathroom.

I managed to make it to the bathtub despite it all and started filling the tub before struggling out of my tank top and shorts. Dipping into the scalding hot water was usually a relief for my aches and pains. I'd suffered from unexplained abdominal pain before and knew many tricks to make it subside, but even after lying still and soaking for some time, I was still in just as much pain. It didn't help at all—very distressing. After ten minutes I realized something more needed to be done.

I crawled, quite literally, out of the bathtub and onto the floor. The vinyl tile under my hands was cold. Trembling, I reached up and pulled a towel off the rack. I felt woozy but I thought it was from the heat of the bath. I wrapped the towel around my body the best I could and crawled on my hands and knees back to the bedroom. I didn't want to wake up the kids and scare them, so I didn't call out to Jack for help.

I finally reached the bedroom and yelled at Jack to get up. He was disoriented, but I didn't mince words.

"I need to go to the hospital."

He was obviously confused. "Why?" he muttered, rubbing his eyes.

"Fuck . . . my stomach. Oh my God, help!"

Fighting through the pain and dizziness, I managed to pull open a dresser drawer and struggle into some underwear and a loose-fitting nightgown. I felt so very woozy but managed to stand, hunched over. In hindsight, standing was not a good idea; the floor seemed to move out from under me, and I fell. It all seemed to happen very slowly, but eventually, the light faded from the outside of my vision inward until it went black.

)(()()(

I wasn't out for long. I woke up in Jack's arms as he sprinted to his Jeep parked right in front of my apartment door. My children, sixteen and twelve and still asleep, were unaware of the ordeal, so Jack locked the door behind us and drove me to Tucson Medical Center just a few miles away.

Riding in the Jeep that night was agonizing. Jack drove fast, and I felt every jarring bump due to the off-road suspension. Pain shot through my abdomen, and I cried and groaned with pain. "It hurts. I'm in pain. It hurts," I kept telling him.

"I'm trying to get you there as quickly as I can," he replied, pulling up to the emergency room.

I couldn't walk, so Jack carried me in like an infant and, scared for my well-being, tried to get me help immediately. A nurse at the reception window rolled out with a wheelchair.

"You can set her down in this," she said, covering me with a blanket.

I could only sit hunched over. Trying to sit up straight caused explosive pain. I cried and squirmed. Only a few minutes passed before a nurse rolled me and my chair back to triage and asked about my symptoms. My voice shook as I spoke through my tears, but I told them about the pain and trembling, the dizziness, and that I had fainted.

Then came the barrage of the usual litany of questions: Are you pregnant? Do you smoke? Do you use drugs? After answering a lot of "no"s, they took my vitals which were, somehow, completely normal. Perhaps because of this, they sent me back out to the waiting room. They told me they'd bring me back as soon as a room was available.

Jack sat with me but said nothing; he didn't try to comfort me, even though I was slumped over in the wheelchair, crying quietly. All I wanted in the whole world was for the pain to stop. So badly.

The waiting room at TMC is usually very busy, but tonight it was worse than usual. Packed, in fact. Despite my agony, I couldn't avoid noticing that everyone's eyes were on me. In a wheelchair in my nightgown, bent over in pain. I felt humiliated. The pain seemed to lessen over time, and then I had an overwhelming desire to sleep. Despite my tendency for insomnia, I just couldn't stay awake. If my mind had been clear, I would have realized how unusual and even worrisome this was.

$$\text{)( )( )(}$$

Four hours went by. A pale and petite red-haired nurse in her forties came through the ER double doors and called my name. Jack pushed my chair as we followed her to my assigned room. Everything seemed fuzzy and covered in a haze of light static as if I was watching this on an old television with a poorly adjusted antenna. Once in the room, I got into bed with the help of Jack and the nurse. While it felt better than the wheelchair, I could only get comfortable in the fetal position. At least with the curtain between beds, I had some privacy, finally, and felt some sense of relief.

The nurse let me know, then, that the doctor would be by to see me as soon as possible but in the meantime, I needed an MRI. By now the clock had swung well past midnight. If I stayed in the right position the pain diminished and I could actually sleep. With that, during one of my waking moments, I told Jack to head home to help my boys get ready for school. I felt like everything was going to be okay and I could handle whatever came next on my own.

A few minutes after he left, the nurse came in and gave me pain medication. I didn't even notice, really, comfortable with my new friend, the fetal position, although it was easier to stay asleep with the help of the morphine. Transportation arrived shortly thereafter; they wheeled my bed to the imaging center of the hospital for my MRI.

Hospital staff transferred me to the MRI table, and the techs asked me to lie straight on my back, informing me that was the position I needed to assume for the MRI to be done. I couldn't even try, so the staff decided to do it for me. What a nightmare! As they tried pulling me into a prone position, my pain skyrocketed and

I screamed and began to convulse uncontrollably. After realizing the hopelessness of their attempts, the nurse gave me another full dose of morphine, but nothing helped. I simply couldn't straighten out my body, and my mind continued to sink, more tired now than ever. Surrounded by exasperated and frustrated staff, with the exception of the sympathetic nurse, I was told that they would go ahead and do the scan with me in the fetal position. At that point, I could not have cared less.

The MRI didn't take long, nor did the two-minute ride back to my room. After what seemed like five minutes, later the nurse came running in.

"Wake up," she said, slapping my cheek a little. "Who is here with you?"

"No one is here with me right now," I said.

I don't remember if I asked why they wanted to know, but the nurse said, "We are prepping the OR right now for surgery. Your abdomen is full of blood."

"What?" I asked. What she said confused me. My mind felt very distant from my body.

She asked if I wanted to call anyone. All I remember was feeling so very tired. I wanted her to go away so I could sleep. I said as much.

"I'm tired, and I want to go to sleep."

The nurse looked at me intently. "You're not tired. You're dying."

She was right. I died that night. Not once, but three times. However, those deaths are not the end of my story. Little did I know then, death can be just the beginning.

CHAPTER 1

THE CRASH OF 2014

Thinking back to the beginning of my career, it was a shit show. I was a few months into my tenure at Child Protective Services, but what happened on this day was a first. I rode in an Arizona state van with two seasoned investigators on our way to a town called Three Points. Well, to call it a town is a stretch. It is a spot on a map, named after its hallmark three-way intersection that included a gas station, a Dollar General, and a lot of trailers without corresponding trailer parks. The long straight stretch of Highway 86, a bumpy two-lane stripe across open desert, churned past us as we rode in silence. I went along with them today for a "learning experience," required by our onboarding checklist. Until that checklist was complete, we couldn't have a caseload. At least in theory. I had one already–building in number. The agency tends to be a bit understaffed, to say the least.

Claire, who drove the van that day, always had her hair up in a tight bun. She wasn't the nicest person and always tried to wear an air of authority. She wore her typical uniform, starched button-up shirts and khaki pants. She didn't share much about herself, but I deduced a fair bit from the bun in the oven, the ring on her finger, and the picture of her husband on her desk. The other woman was not memorable, but I do remember her name–Sonia. She didn't talk much. She had dark hair; a short, stocky woman. I fail to find more to tell.

As we drove, I reviewed the report in an effort to be well-informed when we arrived. It was rather vague, saying that the children were neglected and were special needs, noting there could be abuse occurring and weapons on the property. Also, there could be an excessive number of malnourished dogs with unknown temperament.

It took an hour and a half to get to there from our office in Tucson. We spent the last twenty minutes bouncing along an unmaintained dirt road. Finally, we pulled up to the chain-link fence that surrounded the large plot of land this family lived on. Through the fence, I saw a trailer; a single-wide. It was white, with the door on the end rather than on the side. It almost looked like an industrial site rather than a place where people lived. There were at least ten dogs visible, some on chains, some not, with no shade in sight. Chows, Huskies, some that looked like Labradors. Others that were unidentifiable–mutts, for sure.

Summertime had come to the desert; it was mid-July, nearing the monsoon season. The day would be blisteringly hot, and it started to get humid as well. I sweated through my long-sleeve black top. I was also wearing black capris and black flats. I vividly remember because after I got home, I threw them away.

The gate to enter the property sat closed, but not locked. Two signs hung on it. NO TRESPASSING and BEWARE OF DOGS. No WELCOME sign in sight. We all discussed the situation, the report, and the location and decided we needed some backup by law enforcement. For better or worse, CPS is not an armed enforcement agency. I got out my cell phone and called the Pima County Sheriff Department's dispatch.

After a few rings, a dispatcher answered, "Sheriff's Department, what is your emergency?"

"My name is Rebecca Black. I'm with Child Protective Services. I am calling to request law enforcement assistance for child removal."

"Why do you feel you need officer assistance?"

I described the report we had on hand and the scene in front of us. The combination of the potential danger from the parents, and the obvious ongoing animal cruelty made for a compelling need.

"Deputies will be on scene in five to ten minutes," the dispatch said after I gave them our location.

We decided not to wait. As we were trained, we opened the gate and carefully backed the van in as close as we

could get it to the trailer. Claire seemed a bit panicked–
she was pregnant at the time, and the dogs worried her.
They were quite curious about the van.

The dogs didn't especially bother me, so I said to her,
"Let me get out first and see how the dogs react to me."

She nodded, more than happy to let me do it. I walked
the property just a little bit, to the front entrance of the
trailer and to the east side of it. The dogs were sickly, thin,
showing all their bones: rib cage, spine, hips. The dogs
that were chained had flesh growing over their collars.
They all seemed sad, downtrodden, but none seemed to
pose any threat.

After seeing that all was safe, the other two investigators got out of the van.

"Rebecca," Claire said, "I'm going to knock on the door
and talk to the guardians and potentially serve them the
temporary custody notice. If the report is substantiated,
we are going to remove their children. You can observe,
as a learning opportunity."

She knocked on the door. A lot. Loudly. Some time
passed until finally, the mother answered the door. The
smell of dog shit and piss blew out in a gust as the swamp
cooler in the trailer blasted the air straight at us. Claire
dropped her usual authoritative air.

"Oh fuck!" she said, and then stumbled back down the
stairs and vomited.

The mom's matted hair did nothing to cover her face,
fat and discolored. She was wearing what used to be a

white t-shirt now stained more of a mushroom color. Her khaki shorts had seen better days. She wore no shoes. There were warts and some sort of fungus growing all over her feet, but all over her toes especially. Her toenails were greenish, thick, and looked brittle.

As I looked at her feet, I noticed the floor looked bizarre. It didn't occur to me at first, but I soon realized the floor of the trailer had become something else entirely, now made up of layer on top of layer of dried, petrified dog shit. According to our training, we are supposed to have medical booties that slip over our shoes for cases like these. Not that the State ever stocked their vehicles with them. Shit, I never even saw any in my time with CPS.

Just then, the Sheriff's Department pulled up. As we announced ourselves to the woman at the door, their SUV stopped at an angle about ten feet from our van. Two deputies got out; a man and a woman. They were on alert, with their hands on their service weapons.

Claire said, "I can't breathe."

I offered to go in first. The deputies were behind me. We didn't even make it five feet into the house before we had to walk back out. The deputies offered me a medical mask to try and help with the smell. Of course, I gratefully took it.

"Do you have something to record this with?" I asked.

The deputies walked in behind me again video recording as we went through the house. It was, literally, wall-to-wall dog feces. Some fresh. Some old. Some ancient–turned to rock. It struck me as odd when I saw a refrigerator in the hallway, near the entrance. As I got nearer, it smelled of death. I reached for the handle and opened it. Inside, none of the "food" could be identified. If it wasn't green and slimy, it was wriggling with maggots.

I counted eight more dogs in the house. They were all different breeds, large and small, old and young. While we were standing in the living room, the female deputy made the mistake of standing still, and one of the dogs pissed on her leg.

After some time, we made it to the children's bedroom. In the room stood a set of bunk beds and there were stuffed animals everywhere. Colorful blankets were laid across the beds. It would almost have been like a normal kid's room if it weren't for the omnipresent layers of dog shit.

The two kids, a thirteen-year-old girl and a fourteen-year-old-boy both with Down syndrome were in the room. They, too, were walking through the house barefoot. Their beds had fresh dog feces in spots in the shape of feet and handprints, carried there as they got in and out of bed. They were both covered in dog feces, but they didn't seem to care. Obviously, this had been the norm for them as they grew up.

Sonia worked to help me get the children out of the house. Normally, we could ease this process by letting the children take some of their stuff, things that were important to them. But in this case, we simply couldn't. There wasn't a square inch that wasn't contaminated with feces.

This made the removal process an even greater challenge than usual.

Claire had stayed outside. She spoke to the parents, telling them what would be happening and serving them with the temporary custody notice. It was apparently quite a shock to them that they were living in a hazardous environment.

Once the children were out of the house, the parents became very combative. They tried to convince the children to go back into the house. By then it was late in the day, and we still had to hose the kids off before they could get in our van.

I remember the ride back being awful. Despite our best efforts at cleaning them off, both children reeked of feces. They were both upset, so I tried to talk to them, my goal being to distract them and calm them, but also get information for our report.

"What is your daily routine like?"

"Have you ever felt scared in your home?"

"Has anyone hurt you?"

The girl began to cry and started to shout at me, frustrated and scared.

"My dad touches me where my panties are."

Her brother got very upset and said, "I'm going to get my bow and arrow and shoot my dad!"

It was nearly 7:00 p.m. by the time we made it back to the CPS offices. This was the first and last removal where I didn't have to personally worry about placing the children. This time, it would be Claire's responsibility. I went home that day, took off my clothes on the porch, walked inside and took a shower. I never wore those clothes again.

X X X

That was the first of a long list of awful experiences at CPS. By 2014, two years in, I had developed a bit of a reputation for my lack of fear going into any situation and my ability to pull information from the children and clients I worked with. It put me on my supervisor's radar. He did some research on me and brought me into some cases that belonged to other investigators to see how I performed. Before long he decided I would be assigned to all criminal conduct and Indian Child Welfare Act cases. These were universally recognized as the most difficult cases a CPS specialist could be assigned. I didn't realize it right away, but this would put me in over my head.

Although I felt challenged, and the cases were interesting, they were equally horrifying. This was definitely not the field I saw myself going into when I got my Criminal Justice degree. However, my heart sank into it because in many ways I was the product of a childhood of physical and sexual abuse. And, because I had been wrung through the CPS system myself as a teenager and it failed me, I decided I didn't want to fail these kids. But, because I began to feel in over my head and because I had been through the system as a child, I ended up failing these kids.

There were just too many balls in the air, and eventually, they all dropped.

My case started when I was fourteen years old, but the abuse began well before that. I was born to a schizophrenic prostitute of a mother who had bouts of paranoia and lashed out at me often. As a little girl, she exposed me, out of negligence, to her sexual encounters, as well as, to dangerous situations involving drugs. That was, until, she decided to build a life with my soon-to-be half-brother's father.

Mom got bored easily and left us with him. Starting at age six, he began grooming me, a term or idea that was lost on me at that age. When I reached age seven, I was forced into compromising sexual situations with him, often drugged and raped by him, or gang-raped by his friends. This went on for seven years. Throughout, I was often not allowed to leave my home, my room, or sometimes even my closet.

Working with these children who were often exposed to substantial trauma and lacking love in their lives, all I wanted to do was what was right for them. However, carrying too much of a weight at CPS is a downfall. The more time you took understanding the file, understanding the parents, understanding the trauma the child had been through, and the more you sought to understand the arguments in court, the more behind you got with your caseload.

The timelines, deadlines, and twenty minute face-to-face contacts were all that mattered to CPS. It is as if CPS was all about the numbers and documentation (understandably), but not enough about the actual children. The system is still a failure today, as it was for me back then. As much as I wanted to be there for every one of the children I represented, which averaged just shy of seventy at a time, I began falling apart. With every autopsy report I received, every child I interviewed that experienced sex abuse or had been starved or beaten to the point of going to the hospital, and with the overwhelming number of heinous acts and crimes that made up my caseload, my own trauma began to resurface. I realized that, in the end, I wasn't helping a single kid. Rather, I perpetuated the same system that failed me as a child and caused myself harm all the while. The re-traumatization I began to experience with my daily caseload took an ever-growing toll on my physical and mental well-being, on my daily life, and on my family.

⚸ ⚸ ⚸

My career gradually drained me. The long hours and heavy workload along with the stress and trauma of the type of work I was expected to do led to my being tired continuously, which made me cranky and irritable, and it kept me away from home a lot as I went to work early, came home late often, and sometimes worked Saturdays just to keep up.

Like anything that builds slowly, like gaining weight over time, you don't really notice until it is too late. I went on with my work and tried to balance life, not realizing the toll it took. If you had told me at the onset of 2014 that I would be dead before the year was out, I would have laughed.

Yet, here I am.

Ж Ж Ж

"You're not tired. You're dying," the nurse firmly stated as I struggled to keep my eyes open and focus on her face.

She seemed panicked. She began frantically unhooking me from various tubes and wires because, she said, at any moment the surgical team would be coming to get me. I heard what she said, but I didn't care. My eyes kept drifting. The nurse put her iPhone in my face.

"Is there anyone you need to call?" she asked, tension evident in her voice. "If so, you need to call them now!"

I didn't understand her urgency. I felt tired and peaceful. She kept insisting, though, so I called Jack and told him I would be going into surgery.

"Okay," he said, "I'll be there when I'm done getting the kids ready for school."

I felt nothing, really. I was used to it. Jack is typically emotionless.

Just then, as I hung up, a surgical team of six doctors and nurses came in, but instead of gathering around, introducing themselves and describing the process, they simply ran in and carted me off. When we got to the operating room, they transferred me to the operating table where I remained lying on my left side, in pain. The surgical team attempted to straighten out my body so the anesthesiologist could do his job, but this did not go any better than before with the MRI techs. Perhaps, it went worse. I screamed. I fought them. My body started seizing. The anesthesiologist became frustrated. He didn't know what to do. None of them did.

They had already given me two very strong doses of morphine, but nothing touched the pain. The anesthesiologist eventually grabbed the gas mask and pushed it over my face. His frustrated expression as he held the gas mask in place until I fell asleep was the last memory I had before falling asleep, finally allowing them to position me for surgery.

)(( )(( )((

When I woke up in the hospital room, all I remember seeing is the doctor. In hindsight, I know others were there, but I can't picture them in my memory.

"Surgery was touch-and-go," the doctor explained, standing over me. "We didn't know where the bleeding was coming from so we had to make an incision from sternum to pelvis. The procedure was exploratory."

They discovered that my right ovary had ruptured, a cyst gone bad, so they removed it. "You lost three liters of blood," the doctor said, "and your heart stopped three times."

She went on to explain that I had been clinically dead, not once, but three times that day.

Due to that, they had to put in a PICC line directly to my heart, basically a tube that allowed them to inject things directly into my bloodstream. Obviously, it was all quite overwhelming for everyone there–the crowd I don't remember. All I knew at that moment, disregarding the doctor, is that I wanted to sleep.

)( )( )(

And sleep I did; a lot. I went in and out often through the day and night. The doctors had me on the max dose of morphine they could give me. People came and went, quite a few of them, but most of them were a blur. The ones I do remember were my pseudo-father Russ and his then-girlfriend Roxanne, my best girlfriends Sarah and Danielle, and Jack.

Russ, Roxanne, and Danielle were there almost around the clock, as I recollect, for the first few days. I don't remember what they said half the time, and the other half was typical stuff like "You're looking better today" or "How are you feeling?"

After three days, I was declining slowly but consistently. My vitals were worsening, my hemoglobin levels were falling. Somehow, even though I had lost three liters of blood in surgery, no one thought it might need to be replaced. At that point, I was given my first transfusion (of what would eventually be three). After they put in the first unit of blood, I had to use the restroom pretty badly. The nurses said now would be a good time to do it, before they continued with the second unit of blood. They made me get up and walk to the bathroom.

It hurt, immensely. I was moving for the first time under my own power, out of bed, since the surgery. Pain, both sharp and achy, a big fat, sad face on the hospital pain scale, weighed me down. I walked into the bathroom and turned to face the mirror. Looking back at me was a face, mine but at the same time unrecognizable to me. My skin was grey. Grey! It was horrifying. My lips were literally crusted and white like you see in the movies. The inside of my mouth was white and filmy. I looked dead. I thought for a moment that maybe I was. It was the scariest thing I had ever laid eyes on. I cried. I cried so hard I became dizzy and sick, which really didn't take much.

At some point, my CPS supervisor and the secretary came to visit me. I believe my secretary genuinely wanted to visit me. She was always so sweet to me, but now she smiled and looked a bit sad. In her hands, she held this beautiful succulent, very bright red and green.

I don't remember what she said, but I'm sure it was thoughtful. She was a woman of few words, but when she did speak it meant something—whether she said something good to you, or bad. She had been distinctly overeducated for her position, and equally overburdened at work. I always showed her that I appreciated her–thank yous, brief chats, some candy slipped into her hand–unlike many at the office who treated her as less-than. This helped us get along really well at work. I remembered her fondly and recognized then that I had a lot to learn from her.

My supervisor, on the other hand, walked into the hospital room with no expression–flat as can be–and asked, "How are you?" I am still surprised he even came to visit. He is the type that didn't like to get to know anyone–who didn't want to talk about life or share anything. He wasn't even afraid to awkwardly stare in silence for a few minutes at a time rather than give up something to move a conversation forward. I had this strong feeling that he had to be there for reasons other than to see how I was doing.

I replied, "Fine, now, I guess."

To the best of my ability, I gave him the rundown of what had happened.

"Since you've been in here your cases have been on hold."

I knew it. Asshole.

"I keep an eye on them in case there are any emergencies, but otherwise, nobody has touched them. They're waiting for you when you get back. After you're feeling better, you can get caught up."

When a case is put on hold it means nobody replies to emails or voicemails; nobody makes face-to-face contact with the children; no one keeps in touch with the parents; and no one attends court hearings other than to take notes.

I thought to myself, how would I ever possibly get caught up? I had been in the hospital for two weeks at that point. That may not seem like a long time in the scheme of things, but at CPS that might as well have been a life-time. Two days off sick is enough to throw a case off the rails. Two weeks could be life-altering for the kids I was responsible for.

"Why wouldn't you temporarily assign them to other people?" I asked, exasperated.

"You do so well on these cases. You are on top of them. I don't want to give them up to someone else."

That made no sense to me. Giving the cases to someone else had to be better than having no one on them at all! He must have expected me to jump up out of the hospital bed and get back to work immediately post-surgery. The amount of stress that dropped on me while in the hospital felt overwhelming.

I lost ten pounds in two weeks. On a typically 112-pound person, that is a lot. I still found myself unable to eat at that point. I barely sipped Ensure, under pressure from the worried nursing staff. I constantly felt weak and found it exhausting even to talk. I already stressed enough about what was next, home wise, work wise, life wise. My head was spinning.

Thinking back to that grey woman in the mirror, I wished she actually was dead.

But instead, this was my beginning.

CHAPTER 2

THE MISTAKE

W hen I arrived home from the hospital, things were unbelievably hard for me. My body had changed dramatically–it no longer resembled the body I had lived in my whole adult life. Walking hurt. I couldn't reach for anything. I had to roll in and out of bed, which never went gracefully. My appetite became all but nonexistent. I survived mostly off oatmeal and fruit like grapes and bananas.

I found myself spending long bouts in front of the full-length mirror in my bedroom. My arms and legs were rail-thin. My ass had disappeared. In its place, I found a bloated, misshapen midsection. It had to be wrapped tightly in a medical binder at all times, as my abdominal muscles had been cut in half. Recovering was challenging. As time passed, I seemed stuck, and my mind often played tricks on me, or I felt confused and absent-minded.

I grew quite terrified. I didn't have temporary disability at work. I rapidly drained all of my vacation and sick leave. I needed to do something, and fast, for myself and for my children. We were not safe.

Before long I knew I'd run out of ways to pay for rent, bills, and groceries. Jack had proposed to me about four months before my surgery. He was not, by any means, the ideal guy. He wasn't exactly what I would consider husband material, even at the time. However, I said yes anyway. I was getting older, and I needed help. I had been a single mom at that point for twelve years, and I simply felt done doing it alone. We weren't living together yet since it was my rule that we wouldn't do so until after we were married, but being so unsure about the future I rushed the marriage, in large part in fear for my children. This felt like the only option that would help me find stability quickly. Mostly, financial stability. I know what this makes me. I felt like a terrible person entering into such a transaction with an empty heart. However, growing up the way I did, it was do or die. No–I had two children, so it was just do.

✗ ✗ ✗

Jack and his immediate family were a constant disappointment. A disaster, really. He never helped during the wedding planning, and I'm not even sure he really wanted to get married. Honestly, he rarely seemed to care. "Whatever you want" had been his script, if he even paid attention. More often, his nose stayed in his phone, and a glass of whiskey sat in his hand.

It is not that I wanted to plan some storybook wedding. There was nothing storybook about any of it. It's just that there were a lot of people expecting some sort of ceremony, so I knew we were going to have to come through with something and at a bargain price.

His mom was an alcoholic and a closet drug addict, both pills and cocaine. I learned this as I got to know her and her family. She was a pushy one—she treated Jack like he was her other husband. "Do the dishes!" or "Get that for your sister!" Never asking, always telling. She was not a good person. She even once confessed to me she went to another man's house and spent the night even though she was married. In my opinion, she was fucking crazy. Her main desire in life was to be seen as an exciting, sexual person. It was very obvious to me she had some sort of mental health issue driving her to self-medicate. Blind to all of this behavior, Jack worshiped her. He was, and always had been, in complete denial.

The very first day I met his mother I could tell she was an alcoholic; she drank way too much, got sloppy at dinner, had some verbal outbursts, and then passed out on the couch. What a lovely introduction! I soon found out that was just her norm, though. She pretty regularly fell asleep on the couch after drinking just shy of two bottles of wine.

Jack would often say strange things about her.

"My mom is so strong."

"My friends all think she's sexy."

"She's pretty hot for her age, right?"

She could do no wrong in his eyes.

Yet, she had poisoned him against his aunt, who I found to be just the loveliest person. She was welcoming, forgiving, honest, educated, strong of spirit. I could also relate to her, as she had been a single mother for many years.

Jack's mom, though, had more or less brainwashed all her kids that their aunt was a toxic person. "She thinks she's better than everyone else" or "She's so bossy" or "She never thought you or your sisters were worth a damn" were some of the things she'd say. I didn't see any of that as being true, in the time I knew her.

His father was almost never around, on the other hand. He was a truck driver. The family rarely ever even talked about him. The few times I met him he seemed like a sweet guy. He was, though, totally oblivious to his wife's behavior. I always felt bad for him.

Needless to say, rushing the wedding was, well, a complicated thing to do, and they made it no easier. But I suppose doing so wasn't all bad. I was in pain all the time and had a hard time getting around. I needed a lot of help. Because of the wedding plans, my two best friends were around all the time, especially Danielle. They helped me plan, sat with me and watched movies, sometimes just being present with me when no one else was.

At the time, Sarah was a sergeant with a local law enforcement department. My boys always loved calling her

"Sergeant Sarah," even after her promotion to lieutenant years later.

Danielle was a case specialist at CPS, same as me. She was smart, mellow, and listened well while I often ran at the mouth. When I had a long-winded rant about work, she'd just laugh. My chaotic personality and her mellow one complemented each other well.

Both Danielle and Sarah were busy women, just as I had always been before my surgery. In times of crisis, though, I've learned that the people who truly care will make time. That is how I knew they loved me. They weren't the only two helping me plan the wedding. My friends Russ and Roxanne offered, on short notice, to hold the wedding at their home. The plans were for a small wedding, and they have a lovely yard beside their spacious home.

Russ was a longtime mentor. We'd met through school. At the time he was an educator; a retired judge, teaching law. Eventually, he became my employer. In time, he became like a father to me. I love that man. Roxanne was his girlfriend at the time; they later married. They were crazy in love, truly head over heels, and they made a wonderful couple. Against my wishes, Roxanne insisted on taking on some of the costs of the wedding. I felt overwhelmed and grateful. It made me really glad the wedding planning could be used as an excuse to spend a lot of time with them, as well. I often found myself wishing they were my parents.

Honestly, by the time the day arrived, I actually enjoyed the event. Not the ceremony, but it was May, the tables were wonderfully arranged with yellow or pink roses, the colors were cream, pink and yellow. The bridesmaids wore dresses of pale yellow, and they looked beautiful! It was great to be alive, I looked great, and everybody I loved spent the day and evening there. Danielle, Sarah, Russ and Roxanne, my sons, my brother and his wife, my friend Joe–I was surrounded. Once the sun set, there was candlelight everywhere, and dancing until one in the morning. Everyone had fun, even me. I was able to keep up to some extent thanks to the combo of Vicodin and champagne!

As the night wore on, I felt like Cinderella without a happy ending. The time soon came for everyone to leave. By then, tired and sore, I still hoped there was a surprise ahead. That I would be whisked away to a resort somewhere pretty where I would wake up, and I could sit by the pool. Or something. But Jack had made no preparations for the wedding. He had planned nothing at all. We just got in his car, drove back to my apartment, and went to bed.

The glitz and glitter were gone by the time we got in his car. Midway through the night, the drama began with Jack's mother. The texts started almost immediately, just a few hours after we got home. She explained just how depressing the night had been since tomorrow was Mother's

Day and a reminder of her mother's passing four years earlier.

Jack realized his mom continued to text him several times into the next morning. Despite it being so early in the day, she became cold and obviously frustrated with him that he hadn't responded to her. That he hadn't gotten in touch with her on Mother's Day yet, making it worse.

Feeling guilty and sad for his mom, Jack got me up out of bed to go to the store. He picked out flowers for her and we went to her house to cheer her up. When we got there, she was standoffish, cold, rude. She didn't even mention the previous night. She acted like nothing had happened. She did not even thank us for the flowers.

Knowing we were coming over she decided she was going to go to the gym, on purpose I'm sure. She did things like that quite a lot. Snide things. It always felt like it was meant to hurt me. The Christmas before she got Jack gifts. She got my boys gifts. She nonchalantly said to me, "Oops! I completely forgot you, Rebecca." I think she just didn't like me because I saw her for what she was–a manipulative, lying, drunk, hateful woman.

I should have known marrying Jack would be a mistake. From the beginning, he was a weak person. He was a "yes" man. If his mother, especially, wanted something he'd do anything to get it. And when I say *anything*, I mean things that are beneath the average person. He'd embarrass himself or act pathetically. He tended to be, simply, an embarrassing person.

I was at a low point in my life when I accepted a date with him way back when. Smothered by work, I was lonely and needed a change. He was a car salesman at a dealership where I was friends with the owners. I went there to get a car, and they paired me with him as a salesperson to help me find the right vehicle. I picked an Isuzu SUV. When I went back to finish paperwork, he asked me out on a date. I accepted. The night arrived, and I allowed him to pick me up, although that wasn't my style since I didn't allow my children to meet people I dated unless I was serious. My kids were with their dad that night, though.

He looked, well, awful. He wore a stretched-out V-neck sweater with khaki cargo pants and sneakers. Meanwhile, I wore a dress and strappy heels. We had plans to go to a nice restaurant at La Encantada, the nicest shopping plaza in the city. The place was home to the only Apple store in a city of half a million if that says anything. I looked him up and down, standing in my doorway, and thought to myself that he was quite overweight, with an eager disposition like a chubby kid with a cupcake just out of reach. At the restaurant, we got appetizers and drinks. Without any thought, and with absolute urgency, he ate the entire appetizer before I could even get a taste. He wiped the grease and crumbs on his cargo pants.

It was bad. Really bad, even as first dates go.

Again, though, I was in a bad place. I felt unloved and unwanted. My previous relationship had ended with cheating and lying. That alone would be bad enough, but perhaps worst of all, the guy kept a spreadsheet of everything he paid for and dangled it in my face as things started to unravel.

A spreadsheet, for fuck's sake!

My hopes for love were nil.

As time went by, and we kept dating, Jack's personal behavior didn't change. It seemed as though he continued going through puberty at age twenty-eight. He was perpetually distracted by everything, especially sex and women. He spent most of his free time on his phone, often not listening to me, scrolling through pictures of bikini-clad asses. I would say strange things to him, on purpose, just to hear him respond "Uh-huh." Often it felt like we might as well have been on opposing rims of the Grand Canyon.

He had a whole slew of vices, too.

He constantly blew money. Gambling. Buying needless things. He had no regard for necessary expenses like bills—if he wanted something, he'd buy it, regardless of what we needed to pay. He would often go out at night to hit the ATM for cash so I wouldn't know what he spent it on.

He was also gluttonous, constantly eating. Morning, noon, and night he would eat. Mainly junk food. He'd lie about getting a giant breakfast burrito on the way to work after eating the breakfast I made at home. He'd drink an entire bottle of scotch in two days. He had no concern for his health or appearance. He would just sit on the couch, a lump, playing video games, snacking, and drinking whiskey—often until two in the morning.

He also lacked ambition. I'd often talk to him about taking classes, business classes, to help him advance his career. Or going to school. Doing something besides sales, as it can be a finicky position. He had already decided, though, that he was doing just fine where he was. He didn't want to educate himself, get his body into shape, or tune up his mind. Nothing.

I think I've explained pretty clearly that I knew, from the get-go, that I hadn't made a catch. I did my best to grin and bear it, however. I suppose part of the issue was that I didn't really care. Once my friends and the owners of the dealership found out I was dating Jack, he got a promotion. A big one. He was making much more money than before. He seemed like a security blanket for my kids. In my life, they had always come first.

Things began to unravel, though. Not long after our marriage, I started to lose my mind, and it really had nothing to do with Jack.

CHAPTER 3

THE UNDEAD ME

Once I left the hospital, I found myself home alone all the time. Jack worked early in the morning until late in the evening, and my boys were at school most of the day. We had recently moved into a rental home, almost immediately after we got married. We picked a big house, with vaulted ceilings. It wasn't very old, a cookie-cutter type house in a cookie-cutter community.

Thanks to work, a day wouldn't go by where I wasn't utterly stressed out. My entire body hurt. Doing anything for myself proved a challenge. I kept thinking to myself *Why am I not better yet!?* I tried to take care of the dogs. I attempted to clean the house. I had to dodge calls from my supervisor, constantly badgering me to come back to work. In one voicemail he even mentioned that he intended on assigning me new cases.

That's when it began. The stress levels had been on the rise for, well, since before my surgery. But suddenly a switch was flipped. When I went to bed at night, I started to hear things. Whispering, talking. I'm not sure. When that happened, I got up and walked through the whole house. Everyone was asleep. No phones were lit up. No radios or televisions were on. No neighbors were outside. Nothing to explain it.

After a while I started seeing dark shadows; blobs of blackness in the corners of my eyes, moving up the walls, on the ceiling, on the floor, sitting next to me. I saw them day and night; it didn't matter. I thought maybe it was due to a lack of rest, or perhaps a bad reaction to the anesthesia. I tried to wait it out. Whatever it was. Even though it always freaked me out, I waited; sleepless nights of waiting for it to get better, or worse. But I never would have guessed what I was about to see next.

One of the things I did to try and fall asleep was stare at a solar system of glow-in-the-dark dots on the ceiling that a previous tenant must have put up. You couldn't see them during the day, as it was painted with glow-in-the-dark paint. Only when the lights were flipped off at night did the starry sky appear. At first, I hated it. But over time I grew used to it, and then it became a calming feature at night, especially recently.

One night, Jack and I were getting ready to go to bed.

He said, "Are you ready to go to sleep?"

"Sure" I replied, putting my book down.

He got up and switched off the light that controlled the two lamps by the bed. The stars were there, as they were every night. Tonight, though, they were in the shape of a pentagram.

Were my eyes playing tricks on me? Was my mind? I cried, silently, unable to move. I said nothing to Jack. I didn't trust that he'd understand or know what to do. Hell, I didn't know what to do. All I know is that I was terrified. My eyes were glued wide open until I could fight it no longer. Fatigue drew me toward sleep. I fell asleep crying; scared.

)X)X)X

I was fast asleep later that night when the world around me was shaken by a gigantic *BOOM* in our bedroom. I jumped up immediately and screamed. Jack lifted his head off his pillow and asked sleepily, "What's wrong?" He obviously hadn't heard it.

"Didn't you hear that loud boom?" My heart raced, and I felt panic. It was obvious in my voice.

"No, I didn't hear anything." He was confused, eyes half open, speaking softly. He didn't seem concerned that I was upset. He might as well have asked, "What's the problem with you?"

"You didn't hear the boom? It was really loud! It sounded like it came from right inside here!"

Before he had a chance to answer there was a crackling sound that started in my ears, really loudly. I gasped for air. All of a sudden, shooting up from the floor to the ceiling, three or four feet in diameter, came the most bizarre electric green fire. It made the most unbearable screeching and humming sound.

Out of fear, I backed up to the headboard and stood up with both hands on each side of it. I pressed my back against the wall. I was crying. Screaming, "Go away!"

Within a few seconds, it did. The green flames drained back into the floor. I dropped down on the bed and kept crying with my head in my hands.

Jack asked, "What's the problem?"

"You didn't see that?" I yelled at him.

"I didn't see anything."

I cried harder but didn't say anything more to him.

He said "You are probably just dreaming. Go back to bed."

I never told him what I saw that night. I lay there feeling afraid and very vulnerable. Very unsafe. I didn't feel alive, yet I wasn't dead. I felt stuck somewhere in the middle.

Ж Ж Ж

This left me completely terrified, not to mention completely embarrassed. Who would believe this? I told no one about what I had seen or heard that night. I made an appointment with my primary care doctor, John. When I called, the nurse asked me what I needed to see him for. I lied and said migraines. It worked as a lie because I had suffered from them in the past. She scheduled me.

I came to his office a few days later. When John came to get me from the waiting room and took me back to his office to talk about my migraines, I became hysterical. I cried uncontrollably. I asked if the nurse could stay out of the room.

He got up and locked the door. He seemed concerned. I had known him for ten years, and he had never seen me like this.

It took me a while to calm down enough to even speak. John waited patiently. "Take your time," he kept repeating, caringly.

Finally, I worked up to say, "Something is very wrong with me. I'm hallucinating."

He furrowed his brow. "What do you mean, hallucinating? You see halos and blurred vision when you get migraines?" He hadn't yet put together that I wasn't there for that.

"No," I said, crying softly. "Since my surgery, things have gotten worse day by day. Mentally."

I explained to him that I could hear things. Voices. It sounded like they were right behind my ear, whispering my name. I told him I was seeing pentagrams that I knew weren't actually there, dark shadows moving in the corners of my eyes. Fire, green fire; more electric than natural.

He didn't know what to say at first. This was very unlike him. "Are you taking anything?"

I responded in the negative.

"Have you told anyone else?" he asked.

I told him he was the only one. The only one I could trust.

"You haven't told your husband?" He seemed confused and surprised at this.

I told him no. That I feared telling him because I didn't believe he would understand, or care.

"You need help. Real help. Psychiatric help."

He advised me to talk to my husband, first of all. Secondly, he prescribed Xanax in an effort to relieve some of the stress and anxiety I was under.

The next night I sat down with Jack.

From start to finish I explained the downward spiral since my surgery.

His expression stayed fairly blank. He often didn't know what to do or say in important situations. He'd get this look on his face. His eyes would get big and glossy, and his chin would suck in a bit, a true "deer in headlights" look.

I told him the doctor said I needed to see a psychiatrist. That I needed to seek therapy. That I needed help.

His response was "Yeah. You need to do whatever you need to do."

The discussion, all in all, was very short.

It didn't seem to change his behavior at all. I often found myself wide awake at night, afraid of what might be waiting, crying to myself. He never mustered up the ability to seem sympathetic or helpful, despite what he knew. More often than not, he'd just snore the night away, oblivious to me.

)( )( )(

I knew what needed to happen to get well. I quit my job with CPS. I had to . . . and within a few weeks after some searching, I found a psychiatrist (let's call him Dr. Smith) and a therapist (let's call him Dr. Johnson) who worked together. They were located in the same building, in the same office even. They explained that they worked in tandem, communicating about their patients with each other. The psychiatrist would diagnose me and manage medications while the therapist would help me with coping skills and resolving other issues. It sounded ideal.

When I found these two, at face value, they seemed pretty legit. Both doctors worked in a high-rise building, which is a big deal in Tucson, and they had really well-decorated offices with a staff of people. Dr. Smith was an MD and had been in the field for twenty years. Dr. Johnson, who was just down the hall a few doors, had a PhD in Psychology and had been in the field for fifteen years.

I felt that this could be the start of the right path for me. I began my sessions with Dr. Johnson, going religiously every week, telling him what had been occurring, the visions I was having, the anxiety and fear I felt, and lamented the loss of my independence. He'd stare at me during these sessions with a cold face, taking a lot of notes. Often, he'd turn things around on me, making it seem like things were my fault. He used phrases like "What did you expect?" or "What else was going to happen in that situation?"

He never discussed anything with me—he just listened and made comments. This quickly became frustrating to me. Sure, I knew some of the situations I had been in were my doing, and that they would cause harm eventually. But these things were not done with that in mind. I was never really conscious of my errors until afterward.

It took much longer for me to get into see Dr. Smith. Psychiatrists tend to be much busier than therapists. While Dr. Johnson was a well-dressed man, fit, professional looking and acting, the first time I met Dr. Smith he was twenty minutes late to my appointment. He had a scraggly beard, wore Velcro sandals, khaki cargo shorts and a T-shirt that said LIFE'S GOOD.

I told myself, looks *may* be deceiving.

When he sat down with me, he was frantic. He could not find the paperwork he needed. Giving up, he grabbed a notepad and asked, "Why are you here?"

I explained the same things I had told Dr. Johnson. He jotted down everything I said and pulled out the DSM, the Diagnostic and Statistical Manual of Mental Disorders. I recognized it from my time at DCS, since sometimes we used it when evaluating a child. He thumbed through the book as though he was looking for a definition in the dictionary. He started reading to himself, some of it out loud, none of it discernable to me. After a little while, he looked up.

"Do you often have sex with strangers?" he asked clinically. "Do you spend too much money on a regular basis? Do you tend to be very social?"

He went on with questions like these, which seemed to me to have little to do with hallucinations.

He questioned me for about twenty minutes and then, just like that, he had a diagnosis. "You are borderline personality disorder." He was very casual about it. "Which is typical. It seems to be a woman's disease."

I felt insulted but unsure of how to respond. Dr. Smith was, from all appearances, the expert. He decided he was going to prescribe Topamax. I learned this was an anticonvulsant that is often used, off-label, as a mood stabilizer.

Neither Dr. Smith nor Dr. Johnson, nor even my husband, seemed concerned that I was hallucinating extraordinary things and felt like I was losing my mind. Although I felt heavily discouraged by my first impression of these doctors, as well as by the lack of any real response from my husband, I continued to see my therapist and have regular visits with the psychiatrist.

My hallucinations and more severe symptoms began to decrease. I don't think it was the medication Dr. Smith prescribed, since I stopped taking it almost immediately after I got it. I learned that the side effects were crazy. Hair loss, severe weight loss, long periods of "blackouts" where there would be gaps in time.

The weight-loss side effect was so severe and so consistent that the drug was sometimes prescribed for obese people to help them lose weight. I was, and am, 5'2" and about 115 pounds. I didn't need to lose weight. It would have been unhealthy.

Not to mention I came to decide that not only was his diagnosis shit, so was the medication he was prescribing.

Despite this, and despite the minimal amount of time the psychiatrist spent with me and the very average therapy I was receiving, my symptoms slowly went away.

Slowly but surely, I had fewer hallucinations and heard voices less often. It occurred to me that what had been happening to me was lessening of its own accord and that the doctors I had found were less than stellar. After six months of feeling like I was getting nowhere, I decided to walk away. It was not a good fit for me at that time.

It was not what I needed.

The hallucinations never returned.

It was time for me to find what I really did need.

CHAPTER 4

NEEDING CHANGE

What Jack and I had was the opposite of a relationship. Every time I looked at him, I felt disgusted. I hated him. I hated who he was. How he acted. The things he did. There wasn't a single thing he could do right in my eyes. I felt trapped and lost. And I knew it was my fault. I had chosen him; I had stayed. I had said yes—maybe that's what I hated most of all.

It was in the little things. It's always in the little things, isn't it?

If we went out with people, friends or family, he always had a blank face and acted bored. He was constantly on his phone, usually with his face buried in it. Or, if he couldn't get away with that, it was on his thigh under the table. He could not relate to people. Things never happened naturally for him. He wouldn't come home and greet me like a husband. He wouldn't engage in conversation with me. He never attempted to initiate a relationship with my two children. He just, in a sense, existed.

But, at the same time, there was a side to him that had nothing to do with me. Jack had another life online. Facebook. Instagram. Chive. He'd mostly be looking at chicks, half-naked or naked. Pretty much any app that allowed him to do that from the comfort of the couch, he had installed on his phone. He literally had no control over himself. Toward the end of our relationship, I discovered he had signed up on Tinder. I found out after a while what that app was for. I even found out, while he was showing me pictures of something else, that he had a habit of taking pictures of women on the sly. He snuck pictures of coworkers. Videos of customers he thought were hot.

Bottom line, I learned he was a creep.

I am no warehouse of knowledge, but I was educated. Jack was one of those people who thinks he knows everything because he read an article about it online. He became a joke to me. I nicknamed him "Wiki." It may have bothered him, but he took it lying down, like everything else in his life.

He'd quote things and argue things he'd read online that turned out to be untrue. Everyone proved him wrong. But the Internet and his phone were God. I've never known anyone so detached from the real world. Being with Jack made me lonelier than ever before.

X X X

I needed something. Something different, and desperately. A change. I couldn't live my life anymore, the way it was before. I had fallen apart physically, mentally, and emotionally. I had lost my career. I knew I couldn't go back. The stress I endured working there, the flashbacks it spurred, combined with the fallout of my surgery spelled the end. To make it all harder, I didn't have a single strong person in my life to push me back into the light.

I realized I had been and still was living a lie. I had married somebody I didn't love and whom I had grown to hate. I was trying to be things I couldn't survive being. I had been miserable for a long time, without even realizing it. When I almost died . . . no, did die, and came back . . . the only things that came into my mind over and over again were my children.

A change. I had to make one. I needed to change how I lived, by actually living.

The problem? I didn't have a clue how to get started.

My degree, which I fought hard for while working and raising my sons, was in criminal justice. All of my work experience afterward was in criminal justice. I thought to myself, how can I get away from this field but still keep my degree relevant to what I'm doing? I was very unsure.

However, as often happens in life, an opportunity presented itself. It was small, but it was something. I got an opportunity to teach associate level criminal justice courses at a private college. I taught things like victimology, introduction to corrections and constitutional law, three days a week, four hours per day. Like I said, it was small, but it was something. I really rather enjoyed it. It kept me up on new theories, as I had to read all of the texts myself before teaching them. I got to be creative with my lesson planning. Not only did I get to teach, I was learning. When people want to learn, they also end up teaching.

This started something. It gave me ideas. It connected me to related fields through students' and other instructors' experiences and through the subjects I learned about and taught. One of the big things that helped me in my first career was six years of volunteer work for the Pima County Attorney's Office. It was an opportunity to network, learn, expand my horizons, and be noticed. I figured, since I was working part-time, it would be important and valuable to volunteer again in a related field.

When I was in school myself, one course I found interesting was the Homeland Security course. It was mostly about terrorism prevention, recovery from aftermath, resilience, tactics. So I thought maybe I would volunteer with the City of Tucson's Emergency Management and Homeland Security office. I honestly didn't know much about the underpinnings of emergency management. I really only understood it from my law enforcement perspective which is why I was going to volunteer.

Not knowing where to begin, I started Googling. I Googled everything. Emergency Management. Emergency Manager. There didn't seem to be anything that discussed contacting the office to enroll in a volunteer program. So, I decided just to email the city manager directly. I told him I had just enrolled in a master's program in Emergency Management and that I had a bachelor's degree in Criminal Justice. Mostly, I talked about my desire to volunteer with emergency management for the city. I hadn't actually signed up for the master's program when I emailed him, but I had been looking at it that day, and when I want to do something, I tend to just do it. The following day I was essentially enrolled, pending acceptance, which came a few days later. I actually began classes two days before I started volunteering.

I received an email back from an assistant to the city manager explaining that he had reached out to the city's emergency manager, who had only been with the city for four months but was very bright and capable and would be very happy to have the help of a volunteer. He emailed again later to say Nicolas would be in contact with me sometime that week. Almost a week later, Nicolas called, and we set up a day to meet and discuss details of what the volunteering would entail, daily expectations, and so on.

The next Monday I showed up early for our pseudo-interview, dressed professionally, ready to learn if I could be of any use and if my help was needed. Honestly, I had no clue what I might be doing or what to expect. The City of Tucson's emergency management program is under the fire department, so instead of walking into a dull brick city building downtown, I walked into this completely spic and span, super shiny fire department. It was the city's fire headquarters and everything was so pristine.

I checked in with the receptionist and waited patiently for a few minutes near a glass entry door that secured the rest of the building from the lobby. Then I heard somebody walking down the long hallway toward the door. Since the building was constructed completely of metal, glass, and granite, the footsteps echoed. I was used to working with city or county government employees and know they tend to lean toward being older, past their prime, and generally not well-put-together. But the man belonging to those footsteps looked young. Handsome. Well-dressed. He approached me and asked if I was Rebecca before we introduced ourselves. Then he led me back past the security door into the building proper.

We walked upstairs to his cubicle. The place seemed empty, and it would have been quiet if not for the hum of a vacuum cleaner. Nicolas showed me around the building and rapidly explained his position to me. He spoke fast, showed me around quickly, and then asked me if I had any questions. I felt like I was bothering him. He seemed eager to release me.

I said, "No, not about the volunteer work. But, how many times a week would you ask me to volunteer, and for how long?"

"What are you able to do?"

"Well, as much as I can fit in around my teaching schedule. I have two free days a week."

We landed on a decision that I would come in two days weekly, for full eight-hour shifts.

I was happy and looking forward to starting. Nicolas didn't really seem thrilled, or unhappy. He was pleasant with me, but not obviously excited, so I was apprehensive.

)( )( )(

My first day rolled around. He had me reading a bunch of policy, doing paperwork for my volunteering to make me legit and in order for me to understand guidelines. Typical bureaucracy. I sat in an empty cubicle across from his and often looked up to see him typing something on his computer or texting on his phone. He'd frequently get up and walk the building. He did not talk to me much in the beginning.

One day I was surprised when Nicolas stopped at my desk and asked me to join him for lunch. We went to a Mexican place down the road where he said they had great nachos. It was an odd little plaza with a few random shops, a coffee shop, a sit-down restaurant, and lots of outdoor seating without any shade, which is bizarre in Tucson, but common, unfortunately.

We talked about a variety of things. Nicolas came across as very formal. Thinking back, he was like that when I first met him at work. Lots of "Good morning. How is your day so far?" and "Did you have a good weekend?" I noticed this formality at lunch, as well.

He talked about his career. He talked about his wife and what she did for a living. She was an interior designer. He went on to rant about how people often confused her position for an interior decorator.

"An interior decorator makes things pretty. An interior designer, rather, decides where windows, sprinklers, fire alarms, etc. should go," he said, seemingly proud of her.

When we got back to work that day, being the nosy person I am, I peered inside his cubicle for more details. There were pictures of him and his wife on their wedding day, and elsewhere. There were random pieces of art and lots of paperwork. I remember thinking that his wife was very pretty in the pictures, but honestly, to this day I cannot remember her face.

I noticed that Nicolas often wore professional clothes and neckties, but everything rode the line of hipster. He was trying to be unique, stand out in some way, like his ties. His ties had designs based around barley and hops or engine parts. He even had a navy blue shirt with tiny skulls that you wouldn't notice unless you looked closely.

The next week, I ran late one day and was going to grab a chai latte for myself, so I sent Nicolas a text asking him if he wanted one, too.

"Thanks, but no, I already had coffee," he sent back.

I had noticed every day he'd sit at his desk, typing away, and finish an entire large thermos of coffee. My thoughts started changing that day.

Granted, I'd found him attractive since the moment we met. I knew he was married, and I obviously was as well, but as I was figuring out for myself, that didn't always mean what it seemed on the outside. I was curious about him, quite simply. It seemed he had a façade, especially based on his clothing. But it was not just his clothes. It was the way he walked. The way he talked. The places he talked about going. It all seemed too arranged, too constructed. It was almost as if he was desperate to be something he was not. He seemed so much better than that. It made me want to ask questions.

That's how it began, with the questions.

I asked him so many things about himself.

What kind of music do you like? What's your favorite song? Favorite color? Favorite car?

Where'd you grow up? What are your parents like, and what do they do?

Everything under the sun that I could think of to ask, I asked. Surprisingly, this typically formal and soft-spoken man became more like a sixteen-year-old girl. He couldn't help himself. He began to blab. He told me everything. What he loved; what he disliked. His wishes. Regrets. Things he wanted to do. On, and on, and on. I couldn't shut him up. He transformed. That stiff façade melted away. He smiled! A real smile, not the robotic smile I was used to seeing him wear. He even laughed a few times, something I hadn't seen him do before. To me, that always seemed a bit strange, as I laugh a lot.

He became somebody completely different. From my perspective, he started to become himself. Being the outsider looking in, I don't think he had been that in a very long time.

With all the questions I asked him, there was only one question that ended up being the important one.

Casually, in a text, I asked him one day, "Do you want to get coffee with me?"

I knew this was risky. In fact, it was wrong. Although Nicolas never once said he was unhappy in his marriage, I got the strong sense that he was. As is obvious now, I was utterly miserable in mine. However, I wouldn't want someone to tread on me by seeing my husband behind my back. I felt guilty asking him. However, during our conversations, everything felt so good. So right and natural. It felt like it was worth a little exploration. Anyway, what's coffee between colleagues? Right?

He quickly texted back, agreed, and even suggested a place.

It was a cute little coffee shop on Broadway Boulevard, surrounded by restaurants. Typical for that street, restaurant row, home of every chain you can think of. The shop we went to was a fun little independent one. The plaza around it was full of flowers and nice shops.

We got our coffee and sat at a small table, our knees brushing against one another, and we talked. It was a bit awkward at first. There was tension between us as neither of us really knew what the other was thinking. But the conversation started to flow as we talked about personal things, interests we had. It was enjoyable.

With time, however, I needed to leave to attend to other things I had going on that day. It was the end of summer, and I was wearing a tank top. Before, I had mentioned I had tattoos, a fact which shocked him. I kept them covered in the professional setting. In particular, I talked about my then-favorite tattoo, a Japanese-style tiger on one shoulder. As I was walking in front of him toward my car, I felt his finger touch my shoulder and run down my shoulder blade, going over my tiger tattoo. It was the first time he had touched me. It was a small, delicate touch, but it made my stomach roll around inside me with nervous excitement.

We stopped at my car. He suggested we turn coffee into lunch that our day didn't have to end yet. There was a restaurant just a few doors down from the coffee shop that we could go to, right then.

Surprised by his suggestion, I agreed.

We were seated right away. Sitting there, across from him, I knew from somewhere deep inside of me that we were going to be something. I knew because I already felt guilty.

We ordered some food and sat quietly together for a bit. Nick, as I often called him despite his introducing himself as Nicolas, started talking about spending time together.

"Do you mean as friends?" I asked.

"No, I would like more than that."

I responded, "But, we're married."

He revealed what I already knew. That he was unhappy. I told him I was, too. I confessed to liking him a lot.

"I like you a lot, too," he said.

"I'm not interested in having an affair."

I was clear about that. He said he felt the same way and that he had some open time on Tuesday evenings because his wife went bike riding. I liked him; I was drawn to him from the beginning in a way I can't even describe. I wanted to say no, because it would have been the right thing to do morally. Despite that I said, "We should talk more about it. We should get together again."

I wanted him. That was all there was to it. And I also knew I didn't want Jack, or her, in the picture. I did not want to see him behind anyone's back. This was going to get complicated, for everyone.

CHAPTER 5

IT'S COMPLICATED

The first complication was our working relationship. I was a volunteer working directly for him. When I say it was complicated, it was complicated to focus on what we were supposed to be doing. We often found ways to be close and talk, however, we never focused much on work-related conversations.

Nick was extremely bright. He made me laugh about his quirky ways. The more time went on, I found him laughing and brightening up. He seemed to have shaken some of his formalities and became a man to me, not just a title.

We decided to meet again. We went to a place called the Blue Willow, which is a Tucson fave. Why it is, I can't say. It is not a fave of mine. The conversation was a bit awkward. It was about us finding a way to be together and breaking it off with our spouses. I mentioned I had already told Jack I was unhappy *before* I had even met him, and that I reiterated it again recently, saying our relationship wasn't looking good and was coming to an end.

Nick expressed to me that he was unhappy with his wife and that he believed she was cheating on him with her boss. He felt that's what those Tuesday bike rides were about; she would often be out until four in the morning "riding." He hadn't, however, expressed a plan nor had he confronted her about any of it yet.

I explained to him that if we were to move forward in a relationship, honesty had to be there. We had to be honest with each other, and we had to confront our spouses. I refused to be "the other woman."

Time seemed to speed along. Our desires and intensity for each other grew quickly and were coming to a head. We became more flirtatious at work. He was treating me like I was already his girlfriend. I told him I had asked Jack for a divorce and he agreed. We were still living together, circumstantially, because I was still not working full time and had started school.

That was my next step—find a full-time job and get a place. Jack and I were definitely over. We were both unhappy, and we had agreed to split. Nick, on the other hand, had yet to confront his wife about anything. Not her cheating; not his need to separate. I think he perhaps only mentioned to her that he was unhappy.

Time continues to speed along, as it does when you're having fun with someone. Fun, meaning that we were meeting at the rose garden often, whenever he had spare time, because, at this point, we had decided if we were going to be seeing each other we shouldn't be working together. Just a few months after I'd started, I stopped volunteering so we could see where things were going between us.

We had decided to have our first official date. September eleventh, a Friday. We decided to meet for a cocktail downtown at Reilly's, a hip pizza place with two nice bars.

We both dressed nicely, and were excited and nervous. He ordered something with bourbon, as he does. I ordered something delicious called a lemon drop. It was smoky and dimly lit in the downstairs bar. Everything was old stones and wood beams. We sat next to each other rather than across the table, in the very back booth in the far corner.

Nick, after much time and tension, put his hand on my thigh. Although he did it gently, I felt all the air rush out of me, like in a panic. I went flush. After a time, we decided to leave the bar and walk downtown since the night was beautiful. We ended up on a bridge over Congress Street. There was a big full moon. It was late, with light traffic underneath. We were alone on the bridge with the tops of big trees blowing in the wind around us.

We kissed. It went from gentle and hesitant to intense. We began to grab each other's bodies. He lifted me up by my thighs and held me against the wall; we passionately kissed, unleashing the intensity that had built up over all those weeks from the waiting and wanting.

We walked some more, and in different areas of downtown, we found ourselves stopping to kiss again. I remember feeling like I never wanted this night to end. I wanted him so badly. Finally, we walked back to our cars. We had parked where he worked, behind the secure gate, so they'd be safe. Down in the cool, dimly lit parking garage, we kissed more against my car. I knew we were about to part ways. I wasn't ready.

Without much discussion, I led him into the back seat of my car. With extreme intensity, we made love for the first time. We were relentless. We didn't care if anybody saw. All we could see was each other. Maybe I should have waited before making love to him, but I had never been led by passion before. When I looked at other men in the past, I just saw a list of qualifications. I just saw a secure future or stability. This was the first time I was led by feelings. I realized later this was the first time I'd ever been in love.

We continued our relationship, still in private, as Nick was still with his wife. I was feeling sick. She still didn't know he wanted a divorce. The rose garden was our favorite place to meet. I'd often bring him lunch, and we'd sit under the ramada eating and talking with the smell of roses carried to us on a light breeze.

I rarely got to see him at this point since we no longer worked together. He made every excuse he could so we could see each other, but he found it hard to get away most of the time. I won't lie; I was starting to feel skeptical about whether he was going to leave his wife. *What a fool I am.* There seemed to be so much hesitation and fear, and so many excuses. He'd tell me they had talked a little bit more, on and off, during the evenings about how unhappy they were as a couple. She would either avoid the conversation, or cry, and he didn't know what to do. All I could think is, *You just tell her.*

One day he stopped wearing his wedding band. He hadn't asked her for a divorce yet, but he told her he was unhappy and that things weren't working out. This gave me hope. About two weeks later, though, we met at the rose garden as usual. This time, while I was sitting there, I noticed the ring was back on his hand. My heart sank. Broke, even. *Liar!* was all that went through my head. It suddenly occurred to me that perhaps he just wasn't wearing it when I was around. That he might be lying to me daily. Playing both his wife and me. I was devastated. I jumped off the bench to leave, but he grabbed my arm. He pleaded with me that it meant nothing. He said they'd gotten into an argument that night and that she had forced the ring back on his hand. I found it difficult to believe. If you were being true to yourself, you would have pushed her away or taken it right back off. You'd hold your ground. Like this woman could overpower him. It occurred to me that maybe nothing at all had changed in his home.

I didn't know what to believe anymore. He even told me he still slept in bed with her every night. I was sick. He was ruined in my mind. This man that I cared for so much was just another man. We talked, and I still wanted to be with him, but I also continued to hold my ground. Being that I had never felt that way about someone, I kept seeing him.

At this point, even Jack knew I was seeing Nick. It was almost Nick's birthday. I really wanted to do something nice for him; to get away. It was nothing spectacular, but I booked an Airbnb, a nice little place on the top of a hill with a lot of steps in downtown Bisbee. It was a few hours drive from Tucson. I wanted to spend a couple of nights alone with him, away from everyone, somewhere that we could be ourselves. Where we didn't have to hide.

It was amazing. Sleeping together in bed. Making love. Getting dressed up and going out to eat at a nice Italian restaurant. We woke up that next morning and drank coffee and ate peach pie while watching the sunrise on the back porch. I knew I wanted those things with him forever.

Somehow it came up in discussion how he was able to get away. He said this time he simply said to her he was going to do something for his birthday. He didn't give me specifics; I do not know if he gave her any. He told me that she had desperately tried to have sex with him for his birthday. This poisoned my mind. I started to imagine all the scenarios that had been happening, could be happening, may very well still be happening in his home, with his wife. I hated him for that.

The more my heart filled with love for this man, the deeper the cracks were carved in it. After our trip, we went back to our lives the way they were. Two or three days after our trip, Nick wanted to meet me for breakfast, so I met him at this little place on Campbell Avenue, a new found city favorite. He told me it was over with his wife. He said that when he came back from his birthday trip with me, he realized he couldn't keep doing this, so he left her. He booked an Airbnb for a week and took what would fit in his car. He was so excited and happy.

I asked him if he had asked her for a divorce. He said no, but he was working on it. He looked at me wide-eyed with excitement. He seemed disappointed that I was not more excited, but it just felt like there was still something missing. Either way, I was happy that he was not in her house anymore and that I could see him freely.

We spent many nights together, watching movies and eating Chinese food. He hopped around from one Airbnb to another for about a month. I had gotten a new job at this point, saved up some money, and got my own place. Nick did the same. We each had an apartment.

Nick was avoiding the discussion of divorce. He still couldn't face his wife, and I believed it was out of fear of confrontation. She ended up filing for divorce. Their relationship was ended by default in many ways, but ours had a new beginning.

)( )( )(

Having our own places and being able to spend the evening, night, and mornings with each other, doing whatever we liked—watching movies, cooking together—made it feel more real. As time went on, we lived our lives, worked our jobs and saw each other, but things began to change for me.

I had started working with an agency that helped troubled children, very similar to my previous job with CPS, but more on the therapeutic side of things. I rapidly began to feel stressed, overwhelmed, sick and terrified. I can't exactly describe the feeling, but with each day that passed, I felt as if it was harder and harder to go to work. To get out of bed. To function.

As our relationship grew, Nick decided he wanted to live together, so he moved into my apartment with me. He knew I was struggling, but at the time he didn't quite understand it.

One day, I called him and told him I couldn't go back, that I was stuck on the side of the road, crying. He assured me that everything would be okay and that if it was in my best interest mentally to quit, then he would take care of me until I was better. This was of some comfort to me, but mostly terrifying. I had been here before. *What is wrong with me?*

We sat down together and had a long conversation. He knew about my previous experience after 2014. He knew I had some mental issues. So we decided I should talk to my doctor about what could be done to help.

I took a small break from work and then got a job in retail. Mindless, right? A simple job, something that wouldn't tax me. My doctor prescribed me anti-depressants and anti-anxiety meds, Xanax and Celexa. Time passed while we lived our lives and worked. But at this point, I was having nightly meltdowns, crying, and feeling paranoid. This all started when I left the first job, but it picked up when I started the retail job.

I felt horrible. Nick was always trying to calm me down, make me feel better, hold me, listen to me cry and watch me fall apart. I hated it. I had also started to hate my retail job. The job was selling women's lingerie, so I always felt less-than, but why? Where the hell did all this come from? I used to be a go-getter, at work, school, and volunteering while being a parent. The first part of my adult life was fine as far as I knew. Til the crash of 2014.

This was around the time I started on my new medication. Nick said that if the retail job wasn't the right one for me, it was okay to quit—my well-being was more important. I felt like a failure. I had worked so hard to get somewhere in life and it was all washing away in front of my eyes. My past had ruined my ability to cope with the present.

I was only on the antidepressants a short time when something happened. A side effect, maybe? One day, I felt out of control, like my insides were moving a million miles an hour, along with my thoughts. I felt like I could do anything. I felt angry, happy, and sad all at once. I felt hostile and suicidal. I found myself standing in the rain, crying. Nick came outside and pulled me back in. I looked at him.

"I need real help," I said. "I don't know what's happening to me. I feel like I'm in a dangerous spot."

I didn't know what was wrong with me. I knew I needed to be diagnosed, but my previous experience with psychologists and psychiatrists was not helpful. Through some lengthy emotional discussion, we decided it would be best if I went to the local crisis response center and admitted myself. I knew if I went there I could be observed, interviewed, and maybe get a good diagnosis so I could actually get the help I needed.

We decided to go that day, to not waste any time since I was in such a bad place. It was a strange experience, being interviewed by a caseworker to see if I needed to be there. It was decided that it was important that I stay. The woman interviewing me said I'd be there at least twenty-four hours, but if a doctor advised it, I would stay longer.

They stripped me of all my belongings, and I handed them over to Nick. I kissed him goodbye and walked with the nurse to a room. They had given me scrubs to wear and some socks. After changing, I walked into a room with about twenty other people. Everyone was sitting in strange plastic recliners that turned into a bed. I was told this was unit one, a calmer unit. They didn't feel it was necessary for me to be in the other unit where people tended to be more hostile.

I had never been in a place like this before. It was full of drug addicts, people talking to themselves, people detoxing from alcohol, people trying to start fights. I just sat quietly in my plastic recliner.

That didn't change the entire time. I didn't try to talk to anyone. I didn't get up and walk around. I was wide-eyed and stared at the other people around me, including the staff. I refused to eat several of the meals they tried to serve me. I couldn't sleep. I started to feel panicky as the next day came and I still hadn't seen a doctor.

Finally, the doctor doing rounds came and got me. He pulled me into an interview room and reviewed the nurse's notes and then asked, "Why are you here?"

I said, "I felt like I was at the end. I felt suicidal, homicidal, sad and lost, not in control of my emotions."

He asked me about my past. I told him about my childhood and how I was a seven-year sex slave, often drugged. I told him about my mother—how she was crazy, and beat me, and told me that I was awful and ugly. How, in those seven years, I was a prisoner in a house that wasn't a home. I was often not allowed to go to school, or anywhere else for that matter.

After an hour of discussion, the doctor responded with, "I am so sorry those things happened to you. But the reason I think things like this happen to you is because you're special. You have a light inside you that others don't have. Those people without the light, especially those filled with darkness, see your light and want it. So they take things from you in an attempt to get the light. But no matter how much they take from you, they can never touch the light."

He diagnosed me with post-traumatic stress disorder and told me I didn't belong at the crisis response center and that I would be released that day. He did say, though, that I needed ongoing therapy. I went back to my plastic chair and I sat, taking in the realization that I still needed help. That I needed to find somebody who really could help me.

Four hours after seeing the doctor I was released. I walked out into the lobby with a nurse escorting me and standing there was Nick with a bouquet of white roses. White roses are my favorite. We hugged for what seemed like forever, and in my head, I knew that I needed a new beginning. There had to be a way to start again.

✗ ✗ ✗

Getting the diagnosis of PTSD from the CRC was helpful for my primary care physician. He was then able to prescribe medications specific to that disorder. He decided to prescribe Abilify. Through that medication and Nick's great commitment to being there for me, we survived. It was not easy. I felt paranoid often; depressed; I was having almost nightly crying fits about anything and everything.

But Nick was just always there. He was always holding me, caressing my hair, reassuring me that everything would be okay, that we had each other.

He is the most patient man I have ever met. With every breakdown I had, he was always there with soulful eyes, endless patience, and a heart full of love. He never wavered. He never grew tired. He never argued with me in disbelief, and the more he learned about my life, the more compassion flowed out of him. I loved this man. I knew he was absolutely the one for me.

He must have known it as well, that I was the one for him. When we first met, one of the things we shared was a passion for was hiking. Nick took me to the Tanque Verde Ridge Trail at the Saguaro National Park East. It was beautiful. It was a hot day, and I remember kind of chuckling to myself because Nick was a blue jeans and cowboy boots kind of man. Even though it was hot as hell he was still hiking in his blue jeans, although he did trade in his cowboy boots for hiking ones; I'll give him that. He took me up to a spot on a cliff overlooking the valley. We enjoyed the view, ate some snacks, talked, and kissed. We watched the shadows of the clouds move over the city.

Back to present day: Nick wanted to go on that hike again. It had been a while, and it was one of his favorite spots. It was a beautiful time of year, and it sounded like a great idea. So, we took that hike again. It was cooler this time as it was late spring. We hiked right back up to that cliff. We sat and enjoyed the views. Nick began to talk about why we took that hike again on that day. He pulled a letter out of his pocket. Nick often wrote me poetry. Nick

is a brilliant writer. Nick is a brilliant man. *How romantic,*
I thought, *he wrote some poetry to read to me on this cliff today.*

But as he began to read, not even a whole page into his
two-page letter I knew what he was asking. He was asking me to marry him. He tried to hold back his tears, but
he couldn't. I hugged him and said "Yes!" I kissed him.
He pulled out a beautiful cherry wood box with a white
leather interior and seated in it was a black diamond ring
with a white diamond halo.

It was beautiful. It was perfect. I have never in my life
been a typical girl. I've always loved gemstones, colors,
uniqueness. Status quo has never been me. So, that is
what he gave me, with more than just the ring, which is
why I really said yes.

We began to think of places to get married. We wanted
something simple and private. Nothing fancy. We wanted
it to be intimate and special. We had often met at the rose
garden at the beginning of our relationship, talking, smell-
ing the roses as the breeze blew through them. We discussed
having our wedding there but decided against it.

We talked about somewhere in nature, which got us
talking more and more about an oceanside wedding. We
both loved the beach. Some of that discussion involved
Nick's mother, who had passed before I had a chance to
meet her. She was a lover of the ocean, of whales, of nature.
His family had lived most of his life on the West Coast, so
a thought occurred to both of us.

My best friend Danielle, who used to work alongside me in Tucson, had moved to Oregon a few years before to be closer to her family. We thought it could be perfect. My best friend at my side as a witness, along with her husband. We'd be on a beach, which we wanted. And, it was a spiritual way to have his mother present because we knew the ocean held a special place in her heart.

So, we picked a date at random on the calendar, informed Danielle, and we traveled to Oregon on September 20th, enjoyed the surroundings, ate some great food and had some great laughs. We enjoyed Danielle's family and friends. We went to scope out the location we had chosen the day before our wedding. Lincoln City; an hour and twenty minutes from where Danielle lived. It was fucking cold. The wind had to have been 20mph or more, the air perhaps 55 degrees, plus once we got near the ocean, it was misty and freezing. *Oh my God, we might have to change our plans.*

But we didn't. We stuck with our plans, and the very next day it was sunny, in the mid-70s, with no clouds, no wind. It was gorgeous. It was meant to be. It was September 24th, and I stood barefoot in the sand in front of an ocean sparkling in the sun, holding Nick's hands and reciting vows to the sound of crashing waves. It was a perfect day–it was the best day of my life.

After our brief ceremony, there were a lot of teary eyes, hugging, kissing, twirling me around, and overall happiness. All we had to do after that was walk about a hundred feet to a lovely restaurant with walls made of windows overlooking the beach where we'd just married. We toasted with champagne, just us—myself, Nick, my son Sabastion, and my friend Danielle and her husband. Just as we wanted it—intimate.

The remainder of our vacation was pleasant, with a surprise dinner hosted by the rest of Danielle's family in a casual environment. The entire trip was a blissful experience.

✗ ✗ ✗

Originally, we had discussed that if we got married, we would honeymoon in Australia, or at least somewhere tropical. However, because I hadn't been capable of working since I was unwell most of the time, financially this was just not possible. So we did not have a honeymoon.

We were still living in an apartment together at that time. I was doing everything I could to occupy my mind while Nick was at work. I had never been jobless in my life for anywhere near this long. I was a bit of an overachiever, so to speak.

One of the ways I found to occupy my mind was looking for places to live—a bigger and more comfortable place than where we were. And that's how it came to be. One day I found a house online. It was outdated, but it was in the best neighborhood in all of Tucson—the Catalina Foothills. I had to see it as it was priced so well.

I went alone with a realtor to look at it. Structurally, it was great, but the inside definitely needed a lot of work. The kitchen, bathrooms, paint colors and flooring were all outdated. However, it had a magnificent brick double-sided fireplace, easily five feet long, dividing both living rooms. There was also a very large atrium–I saw the potential for a peaceful garden inside the home itself.

But the best part of this house was the back garden. It was very full and green, rich with different kinds of colors, flowers, and rose bushes. However, the best part of all was that this house sat on top of a hill with a wash running behind it all the way down the hill. Nothing had been, or ever would be, built behind us. This left the house with a southerly view of the entire cityscape. During the day, it was spectacular–I could just imagine what it would be like at night.

Anybody who knows me knows that when I want something, I want it until I get it. I threw the idea at Nick. He is not the same as me. He likes to think about things, mull it over, compare, contrast, all of the above. I'm a "Yes, let's do it!" He's a "Let me think about it." We balance each other.

Needless to say, I pushed. I showed him the photos–he wasn't that impressed, but he liked the fireplace, the price, and the location, so I was able to convince him to look at it. We walked in, walked around, and made some jokes about the parts of it that were painfully outdated.

However, he saw some potential in it as well. I explained the things we could do, that I wanted to do, which put him in the same mode of thinking. And we both were on the same page about how nice it would be to have a house.

Nick being Nick, however, he wanted to see a handful of other properties in a similar price range and in the same general area before deciding. Considering the price range of the first house–the house I had fallen for–the other houses we saw were a shit show. It was one dud after another, a mix of disappointment and disgust. We quickly learned the first house was an overlooked gem.

Finally, after seeing the house a few more times and thinking about all the benefits, Nick bought it for us. I had no job and terrible credit, so I couldn't even be on the loan. But he loves me so much and trusts me as I trust him, so he put both of our names on the deed. It was now our home and we were so excited!

I had an abundance of energy as we moved in at the beginning of December. Christmas is hands down my favorite time of the year. I knew I wanted to make the house at least bearable to live in by Christmas time so we could enjoy it.

So every day, in the beginning, Nick and I did some painting, changed door knobs, installed new faucets and appliances. Nick took a week off work after moving in to do projects, and after he went back, I kept on trucking, painting, doing projects, and everything else I was capable of.

)( )( )(

As Christmas approached, we found ourselves a tree and decorated it. It was a minimal year for decorations since everything was so rushed, but we were so happy and proud to be having our first Christmas as husband and wife, and our first Christmas in our new home, together.

Sometime around Christmas or perhaps just after, Nick and I made a bed of pillows and blankets on one side of the fireplace. All of the lights in the house were off. The fire was roaring and crackling, and we held each other and watched the flickering lights of the flames. After some time, we made love and then fell asleep in the warmth of the fire. I think that was the first time I truly ever felt at home, in my heart.

Although things were going well, and in fact seemed perfect with the new house, our new marriage, the projects we were doing and my new sense of safety, something was still very off. I'd find myself crying for no reason, feeling manic at times, feeling depressed just as often, and struggling with frequent flashbacks. Obviously, I was not cured. It was apparent to me that I needed help; wanted help. I didn't want to ruin this new life I'd started.

CHAPTER 6

GANESH

Ganesh—although he is known for many attributes, Ganesh's elephant head makes him easy to identify. He is widely revered as the remover of obstacles. The patron of arts and sciences, and of intellect and wisdom. As the god of beginnings, he is honored at the start of rights and ceremonies.

I began a search. I was looking for a psychiatrist as I knew I would need therapeutic help, but also medication management. It was not easy. After many days of phone tag, when I could finally get someone on the phone at one office or another, I'd learn that they either didn't take insurance or that they didn't treat people with my symptoms. I was made to feel like my case was too difficult.

Feeling like it was going to be impossible to find a psychiatrist, or to afford one in any case, I decided to look at therapists. I figured it would at least be a start. I found a few, but one specifically who had availability right away and would take somebody with my symptoms. In fact, they stated that they specialized in the treatment of PTSD.

My first appointment with this therapist was strange.

He was a rather nice guy but distracted all the time. He'd get caught up in his own thoughts, have a small rant about something, or feel the need to tell a personal story related, or not, to the topic at hand. The second time I saw him, he was about ten minutes late, venti iced Starbucks in hand, and it took him several minutes to get situated in the office before we could even start our session.

By the third appointment he had bought himself an espresso machine for his office, which he was quite proud of, but he was still ten minutes late. He talked about his espresso machine for a good ten minutes of our session and got distracted by making himself more during our session.

Overall, despite his kind disposition, he was chronically late, constantly distracted, and obsessed with his coffee. I couldn't help but focus on his issues, because I knew he wasn't focusing on mine. Not really.

And beyond all of that, when he prompted me to talk about my childhood trauma, and I told him a story involving my mother and the man who sexually molested me during my childhood, he became overwhelmed and a bit emotional, which felt uncomfortable. Plus, we hadn't even scratched the surface, and he was already struggling. I was supposed to be the one having a hard time!

After deciding to cut ties with this therapist, I remembered something my P.A. John suggested to me during one of my doctor's visits. He said I might find a psychiatrist to work with at the local university if I was lucky enough to get in without a long wait. Most people have to wait for months, as he explained. So I called the university psychiatry department and explained that I was hoping to be seen, become a new patient, and that I would be looking for ongoing care. I was put on hold for a few minutes. We discussed insurance briefly. Then, I was told I was lucky—there was a doctor, a new resident, who was opening up availability to see new patients. I would be able to see him in about three weeks. She said it would start with an evaluation and I should plan for that to take ninety minutes to two hours.

✗ ✗ ✗

Having followed through on making an appointment at the local university to have a proper evaluation done by an attending and resident psychiatrist, I now found myself waiting anxiously in the lobby, not really knowing who or what to expect in this new situation.

I had to fill out a huge packet of info; history, symptoms, diseases, you name it. Above and beyond anything I've dealt with at a doctor's office before.

Finally, after what felt like forever, I was called back into a room where I met Dr. George and his attending. The attending explained to me the evaluation process would take about ninety minutes and we would discuss symptoms I'd been having, reasons I felt like I needed help, and any current traumas or diagnosis, etc.

The attending was very well-put-together, dressed neatly, but plainly, and spoke calmly. He was an older, stocky man with white hair. He seemed sweet and kind in the way he questioned and spoke to me. When he was listening, I could tell he truly heard me.

Dr. George, on the other hand, seemed fresh and new and a little unsure. He seemed to let his attending lead the procedure. When his attending referred to him to see if he had questions, Dr. George would pause and seem a little off guard. He'd ask follow-ups to questions his attending had already asked. He was a little underdressed, and not put together all that well.

They proceeded to ask me why I was there. I began to go through a long list of symptoms. I explained that I went through severe trauma as a child–brutal physical abuse, sexual abuse, emotional abuse, medical neglect, malnutrition. That I had been a CPS child, and that all of that had never really bothered me past a certain age. I had been able to go to college, get a degree, have a life and raise two boys.

I explained, though, that in 2014, I almost died. With that recovery, my whole world came crashing down. I had hallucinated; I was paranoid and anxious constantly; I'd cry daily, sometimes several times a day; and since then it had dwindled a bit but now had become more complicated. It had developed into manic and depressive episodes, night terrors, flashbacks, all leading to an inability for me to maintain employment, to be a supportive, healthy, happy wife or a good parent.

I told them I believed the trauma of the surgery in 2014 somehow opened the floodgates of all the trauma I had experienced in my life prior to that day. That it unleashed something in me that I no longer had control over. They listened intently and asked a lot of follow-up questions about history of mental illness, more specifics about the symptoms I had been describing, other things that may be happening I could have missed and things that had happened in the past.

Worst of all, though, in order to understand the depth of the trauma I had lived through, they said they needed an example of some of the most severe trauma. So, I picked a memory.

To me, it was the first time I was officially broken as a person. I was no longer a struggling child, much less a child at all. This memory was of my perpetrator drugging me with a handful of Valium when I was seven or eight. Feeling scared, I passed out pretty quickly as things began and later woke up on the floor of a closet, naked, filthy, and bleeding. It was the hardest thing I ever had to say to anybody. It was rare that I ever vocalized any of those memories. They just lived inside me.

The psychiatrists thanked me for sharing that memory with them. They needed to discuss something and that they would return in a moment. When they left the room, I realized I was crying.

XXX

Some time later they returned.

The attending said, "We would be happy to treat you. I'm so sorry all this has happened to you."

He went on to explain that Dr. George would be my doctor and that he would oversee my case as Dr. George was a resident.

The attending made a comment. "Your case is going to be a difficult one. We both sincerely hope we can help you."

They gave me a diagnosis which they believed was accurate at the time but said it could change with treatment and as they learned more. They diagnosed me as bipolar two with post-traumatic stress disorder.

Dr. George explained, "When we start our sessions, we will talk more about your diagnosis, what it means, what kind of medications can help you. After we're done here today, we will put together a treatment plan, but you and I will work on that more together to make sure it works the best for you."

He seemed genuine and caring, but also a little nervous and unsure. Perhaps because I was a new patient to him, or maybe because he was a new doctor. Either way, we parted.

As we said our goodbyes Dr. George said, "I look forward to working with you."

I was scheduled to see him weekly from that point on.

※ ※ ※

One week later, I went to my first appointment with Dr. George. My first one-on-one with him was different than the evaluation. He took me back to his office, which was private, dimly lit, his desk a bit of a mess. He had random personal items on his bookshelf, but otherwise it was filled with medical textbooks, theory books or guides. It smelled a bit like some sort of incense or fragrant oil, though I couldn't place it beyond that. He looked like he had just rolled out of bed and simply thrown something on before rushing to work. He seemed disorganized and exhausted. However, he was attentive and wanted to hear more of my story.

"Tell me about your daily life," was one of his opening prompts.

We discussed a bit what that looked like, which helped give him an idea that I didn't sleep much and that I was stressed a lot. He decided, based on what he learned about my daily life, that my lack of sleep was a big concern. We all function better on sleep, regardless of any other diagnosis. So as a starting point we focused on me finding a way to get better sleep. Otherwise, our session was focused on him learning more about my life, my experiences, and my feelings.

Overall, Dr. George came off as thoughtful and caring. He never once looked at the clock while I was there. I didn't feel rushed. I felt like he was genuinely interested in my story beyond just his professional duty and that he really wanted to help me. I thought my first session with the rather scattered Dr. George went very well.

✕ ✕ ✕

After leaving my first session, I found myself returning to the usual me: cynical. I wondered if first impressions were something he did well. Was it really genuine? I began to second-guess everything. I spent the whole week obsessing over what I had told him. What I would tell him next. What he would be like next. These are typical behaviors for me. I tend to see the dark side of things. I tend to be cynical. A tendency for doubt and mistrust definitely comes naturally to me, and paranoia is definitely at the top of the list of the things I'm great at. Always paranoid about what people thought of me. Paranoid about what people are up to. Paranoid about what people are like behind closed doors.

I never truly trusted anyone.

I finally made it to session two. There he was, Dr. George. A little disheveled in his appearance. His clothes didn't quite fit him. It looked like he had just rolled out of bed again, or perhaps he hadn't gotten any sleep at all. A can of Monster sat on his desk. I found myself thinking that I couldn't believe he drank that crap.

Nonetheless, he was kind, professional, and again he never looked at the clock. There was no prompting of a session nearing its end. He never made inappropriate comments about things I was saying, nor did he push me too hard. He seemed as if, maybe, life for him was chaotic. Within the four walls of his office, though, regardless of my emotional state, I found it peaceful. He was attentive; whatever chaos may have been happening to him outside those walls stayed outside.

I was impressed by that.

I have never worked with a professional in any field that was so capable of keeping everything out–personal and work did not mix. Period. He was completely focused on what was happening there, with me, in every moment.

As time went on, we discussed many things. Of course, it started out with why I was there, what I was feeling, what behaviors I was exhibiting. We talked about a summary of my life, light on the details. After a while though, we reached a point where I asked him–"Is discussing the trauma in my life the only way to make these flashbacks, these nightmares, these insecurities and disruptions in my life go away?"

"That's one way." He went on to ask, "Do you want to discuss your trauma?"

"I can talk forever about the trauma that happened between my mother and me," I said. "She was violent and crazy. She often beat me with things and hurt me. She ripped hair out of my head; burned my scalp with hot water making my hair fall out; starved me; neglected me. She had sex with people in front of me. And on, and on."

However, the sexual trauma I found almost impossible to verbalize. It was like I'd freeze up inside and feel sick. The idea of somebody, someone who is good, knowing the disgusting, awful things that happened to me horrified me. I liked Dr. George. I respected him and felt he was a good person, even though I was still getting to know him. How could I say stuff like that to him?

Then there was the whole idea of actually hearing myself say it all out loud. I remember one session when we were discussing a variety of things when one thing came up about a flashback. It was prompted by something that had happened in my current life. I was in a bad place, a low point, and my husband was holding me. He grabbed the back of my head and started stroking my hair, and I freaked out.

It was like I was back there again. I told this to Dr. George.

He asked, "Why? Where did it take you?"

Almost without realizing, without control, I began shaking my head. "No," I cried. I didn't tell him. I couldn't. As our sessions progressed, I hated therapy. I cried often. I said things I didn't want to say. I exposed myself. Most of all, the one thing Dr. George emphasized more than anything was that I allow myself to be vulnerable.

Although that was good, in his opinion–progress, even– I hated it. But I only hated the feeling of it. I realized I actually felt safe being vulnerable with him. That was a big deal. I didn't like to be vulnerable for anybody, and when I was, it was never comfortable.

)K)K)K

As time went on, I became more and more comfortable seeing Dr. George, and I realized that this was a unique experience. In the past, I'd been uncomfortable with therapists, psychiatrists, anyone who was trying to help me emotionally. They were always taking notes, looking at their watch, setting a timer, watching the clock on the wall, and talking more than I did. This was not the experience I had with Dr. George. He was patient, quiet most of the time, attentive, and as I've said before, he seemed unaware of time.

I realized rather quickly that he was notorious for letting us run over our time by a half-hour, pretty much every session. In fact, I learned he scheduled me for times when he had no appointments afterward just so we could run over if needed.

We began trying different medications. Stuff to help with anxiety, sleep, mood—it was definitely a process, and he paid close attention to what was going on symptom wise to make sure I was always safe. Some things helped, others didn't. Mostly because I reacted to them poorly. My body seems to be sensitive to medications, with the exception of benzos—Klonopin, Valium, etc. I could take a handful of those and be fine—not that this is what he ever recommended or prescribed. I found Dr. George was very delicate in the way he prescribed. He always started very slowly. He was very cautious. He often took breaks from things before prescribing new medications if something didn't work well for me.

My appointment day became regularly scheduled for Thursday at 4:00 p.m., for an hour. This meant that when we ended, usually well beyond the one-hour mark, the building was closed, at least for that department. Since we often ran over, it usually felt like we were the only ones that were ever there. I honestly began to feel like maybe I was his only patient. I knew that wasn't true, I knew he had other patients, but that was the kind of doctor he was. He made you feel cared for, beyond the usual sense—not just as a patient, but as a person.

Overall, in the first few months of working with him, I was sold. He had built trust that no one else in that setting had ever been able to build before. He made me feel his compassion. He was patient. Perhaps most of all, he never used anything I said against me.

I was committed. This was it. He had to be my permanent psychiatrist.

Ж Ж Ж

Although working with Dr. George gave me perspective, and the medications began to help, we always focused on day-to-day life at this point. Obviously, this is where my practical difficulties lay, but there had always been a reason behind them. A reason why I had to live with these difficulties. The problems stemmed from the past.

Every day I saw him I could tell by the look on his face that he expected more. He expected me to share more. I knew that eventually, I would have to start talking about the elephant in the room. This elephant was huge. It was my sexual abuse history. Talking about that had never been easy. How could it be? Where do you begin? How much do you tell? What is relevant? I was terrified.

I started back up again with a similar story to the one I provided in the beginning when they did my evaluation. I was force-fed a lot of Valium. I told him, thinking back on it now, being a child and forced to eat 10mg pills of Valium in quantities of five or six pills could have killed me. And that, sometimes, I wish it had.

I told him that as things began that night I fell unconscious. It was a group thing. Something I learned as I got older and studied criminology is that pedophiles know one another. I was sprawled out on a poker table being stored in a room along with other random gambling tables. Luckily, I don't remember any of it. Just how I woke up. It is hard not to feel disgusted with yourself when waking up in the conditions I did. This is why it affects my everyday life. Humanity is a strange thing. Why it is called humanity is even beyond me. Experiencing all the things I did, learning all the things I learned in college, and then doing the job I did, it felt like there was nothing humane about people at all.

I explained to Dr. George this is why I left my former career, had my crash of 2014, went through the various jobs I tried and failed to hold down in between; it was all because I knew I needed to find something I was truly passionate about. Something that brought me joy, happiness, and helped correct my perspective on the world. He agreed that was a healthy goal. But what did that mean to me? What in the world could I be passionate about beyond what I originally thought I wanted to do?

He directed me to explore what sorts of things interested me.

"It could start with something simple," he pointed out, "like taking a class, or volunteering."

Basically, I was trying to find a new niche in the world. I agreed to be open-minded and think outside of the box. To go beyond my typical governmental, criminal justice oriented qualifications. Not that they were even useful anymore.

Admittedly, I was frustrated. Everything he said to me made sense, but here I was, thirty-seven years old at the time and I found myself in a position of starting over from scratch. Still, I left his office that day on a mission. A mission to try and find something I hadn't thought of before. I knew it was going to be a challenge to figure out where to start.

CHAPTER 7

MEETING THE ELEPHANTS

I had chosen a path and walked so long and hard down that road–graduated with a degree, volunteered for thousands of hours across various organizations in government, built up my resume, networked and made a name for myself–only to fall off the edge of the earth when it comes to the world of criminal justice.

I had a government job. I volunteered for the Pima County Attorney's Office with 88-Crime for close to six years. I went through the FBI Citizens' Academy. I worked closely with the US Marshalls Service to re-release its Most Wanted program and even spoke at a press conference with them. I worked hard to make a name for myself in that circle in Tucson and beyond. Now it was all over.

Having no other experience, at least not in anything I thought I would be interested in, it is hard to know what to do, career wise. It is hard to know what your passion is when you thought you'd already found it, only to have it taken away.

It is easy to know what you love in your day-to-day life. I love flowers, so I thought about working at a nursery. But no, it would be hot and boring, and overall I thought it was just a stupid idea. I love decorating, but you actually have to specialize in that, and it is a hard job to build a name in. Plus, I only love decorating my house with the oddball stuff I like! I can't say I'd have enjoyed decorating some stranger's house to fit their ho-hum taste.

I love art, but I don't have a degree in it so I couldn't teach it, and I can't paint for shit.

I felt lost. I didn't know what I was passionate about. It was almost like the universe, the angels, whatever you look to when you're lost, heard me calling for help, and then help arrived.

My son had a friend he'd gone to school with for years, and one day his mother mentioned volunteering. I told her I had mostly volunteered in government. She had volunteered mainly in the arts. However, we shared something in common, and it struck her one day.

She said, "You love elephants."

We both had different elephant art around our homes and discussed our shared sense of their spirituality. She mentioned that she had volunteered at the Reid Park Zoo for a brief time working with the elephant team.

I asked her, "How is it possible to do that?"

She said, "I just applied and interviewed. They either select you or don't. Nothing complicated."

I mentioned that elephants were important to me, but it went beyond that. When I was a little girl, whenever I saw anything elephant related I simply had to have it! They were so precious to me.

When I was fifteen years old, I had an intense dream.

I was lost. It was very dark. My eyes slowly adjusted and I could just make out tall, thick shapes all around me. Trees, perhaps, or the giant legs of monstrous creatures. The sounds of water droplets landing on dead leaves accompanied me as, cold and scared, I wandered aimlessly through the night.

I do not know how long I wandered, but somewhere far above, it seemed as though the sun had risen. Thin tendrils of light dripped down through holes in a distant canopy. I learned I was lost in a jungle. Dripping wet trees and vines surrounded me, darkness the only thing to be seen as I tried to look between them. Strange, unknown animal noises hung in the humid air as the world around me awoke.

I didn't know how I had come to be there, only that I was completely alone and a bit desperate and scared. The meager light filtering in now did not help me find my way. I wandered aimlessly. A cool mist drifted around my feet, hiding the twigs that occasionally cracked under my footsteps.

As the day waned, I resigned myself to wandering in this jungle until fatigue and dehydration took me. I cried out for help, only to be answered by otherworldly screeches and moans. Eventually, I came across a downed tree. I sat, resting my feet. A few minutes passed as I let my mind wander, looking up at a glimmer of sunlight that, to my eyes, was the size of a coin. Then, suddenly, a twig cracked behind me. I whipped around, screamed, and fell backward off the log, thumping onto the ground, my fall broken by inches of dead leaves.

It was an elephant! It seemed to have appeared out of thin air. If it had walked into the small clearing I sat in, it certainly had done so silently. I stood up, and it was now directly in front of me. We were face-to-face, though a mass of dripping leaves on a branch projected from a nearby tree filtered my view. Despite my shock, I remember instantly feeling safe and calm. It reached toward my hand with its trunk. I held its trunk in my hand, and I didn't want to let go. The elephant, however, had other ideas. It turned around and, silent no more, crashed its way through the jungle. I frantically followed, and in time, my elephant guide brought me to the edge of the jungle. To safety.

The dream felt like it had some sort of meaning. It was one year after I escaped captivity–escaped my abuser. I was more lost than ever, though–a runaway, trying to find my way through a system stacked against me. Even though it was a dream, it was the first time I'd felt peace or safety in a very long time. It stuck with me.

For these and other reasons, elephants are important to me; they are different from other animals. Even before I found out about this opportunity at the zoo, I'd taken every opportunity I had to read about elephants or watch documentaries on them. I even went to every zoo in every state or city I traveled to, just to see their elephants. I found them spiritual, ancient, even holy.

)( )( )(

Knowing now that I could apply at the zoo to work with the elephant team, as soon as I could, I went online to check it out. I was disheartened to see other volunteer positions at the zoo were open–but none for the elephant team. I applied anyway, to be a docent or part of the education department. I figured it couldn't hurt to get my foot in the door. However, in the notes section, I wrote that as soon as an elephant position opened that is what I would prefer. It took a little time, but the volunteer coordinator got back to me. She said there actually was a position with the elephant team and invited me to apply. I was surprised and excited!

I felt so very happy.

"Absolutely!" I said.

She gave me interview dates, and I selected one.

I arrived promptly that day, and was very excited. The volunteer organizer, Carrie, was doing the interview. She asked me some general questions about myself, my life, what I thought of zoos, animals, and conservation. Then she asked me if I would be opposed to working in the sun, or in the cold, shoveling and raking and doing other difficult physical work. I love physical work—it leaves you feeling accomplished—and I love the sunshine.

She wrote some things down as we spoke. She had a smile on her face the whole time, as did I. She said she would be consulting with the elephant team and that she'd get back to me.

I was extremely hopeful. I felt almost sure of getting it!

Not much time passed before Carrie reached out to me and asked when I could start. She informed me about what I would need to bring, and that a zoo volunteer shirt would be provided when I arrive. She noted that the first day would be a trial day.

"Some people just don't quite understand what they are getting into when joining the elephant team," she explained to me. "Despite saying they are okay with the hard work, it is not unusual for folks to step away after day one."

⯊ ⯊ ⯊

It was early February when I started, around the first week. It was very cold that morning, but I came prepared.

Timberland boots, tactical pants, long sleeve shirt, gloves—I was so excited!

As instructed, I walked through the back entrance and into the meeting room where the keepers met each morning.

Quite a few keepers and volunteers came in. Then Carrie arrived, and the meeting began with a discussion of the day's need-to-knows from around the zoo. Then Carrie introduced me to one of the elephant keepers.

"This is Meghan," Carrie said.

Meghan was a young, tall, blonde woman who was decked out in the standard-issue zoo khaki tactical attire. Fully equipped with a hat to fend off the glaring sun, and her hair pulled back in a bun, she walked me back to the elephant area.

"It's nice to meet you. We are going to start on the elephant yard first. That's where we always start. You'll need two tools every day–a rake and a pick."

After she instructed me which tools to bring along, we walked past the barn. This was the inside living area for the elephants, as we walked by, I could see all of them! It was quite the sight; a whole family of these beautiful creatures in one place.

There was another volunteer with me by then, a man named Richard. We walked into the break room where we stored our personal belongings. There, I met Cassie, the elephant team lead. She had a kind face and was smiling. Decked out in the same attire, wearing a big sun hat that was contrasted by the pearl necklace she wore, she gave off the air of being tough, but feminine.

After introductions, she told me, "You'll be paired up with one of the keepers just for a short while until you get the hang of it."

The other volunteer who was with me, Richard, was retired military, perhaps Air Force. He had been with the elephant team as a volunteer for three years.

Cassie said, "If you get lost you can just ask Richard."

Out to the yard we went. We had seven acres to rake and shovel up. Our job, I quickly learned, consisted of three tasks out in the yard–pick up all the chewed on branches and logs, rake up every bit of hay on the ground, and make sure there was no trace of elephant dung!

This was to be done over the entire seven acres. It was a fast-paced task! The clock was ticking as patrons would be coming soon, looking to see the elephants out on the yard. It had to be cleaned and refilled with treats, food, and fresh branches before then.

It was quite a task, to say the least. However, we weren't done yet. Once the seven acres were cleaned completely, the elephants could be shifted from the barn where they spent their nights, into the yard. During the shifting, the volunteers cleaned up the hay barn, hosed out the trucks, and prepared and cleaned them to be filled with food. Once the elephants were shifted, it was our turn to be shifted back to raking, shoveling, and picking up branches but this time in the paddocks.

The paddocks were the outside holding areas. Once the paddocks were clean, we moved to the inside barn. These were huge air-conditioned, holding areas for the elephants. Guess what? In there we raked, shoveled, and picked up branches!

When that was all done, if we hadn't quite met our four hour time for the day, we were to sort "brows." I learned these were what the keepers called the branches that were fed to the elephants. Regularly, a big truck would come and dump a gigantic pile of ten- to fourteen-foot-long branches and giant logs, mostly from mesquite and acacia trees.

These giant, tangled, mixed-together and thorn-covered branches had to be pulled out of the mass—which took a lot of strength at times—and sometimes had to be cut down into shorter pieces. Then, they had to be closely examined.

First, were the thorns too large? If so, into the trash pile they went.

Second, was it infected with mistletoe? If so, trash pile!

Third, we had to sort them into common piles by type of tree. These consisted of mesquite branches, acacia branches, leafless logs, medium-sized logs, and a standard stick pile.

This was just a standard expectation of an elephant-team volunteer. There were so many other duties that could be included, depending on the day.

In February, the hours for zoo volunteers ran from 7:30 to 11:30 each morning. However, since I was new and needed somebody with me most of the time, my first day they let me go home at 10:30am due to a lack of staff to chaperone me. That said, they told me I had done an exceptional job, and they would be excited to have me back.

I had passed my trial day. I was thrilled to be an official elephant-team volunteer!

I came home that day absolutely filthy, drenched in sweat, totally exhausted—and filled with joy. I took a long, hot shower and then I called my husband at work. I was so proud and excited to tell him that I had passed and that I was in as an official volunteer. He was not surprised.

"I knew you could do it!" he said.

He was happy for me and reminded me that I could do anything I wanted.

)(( )(( )((

I started by volunteering just one day each week. Quickly, though, I wanted more! That one day a week felt so very far apart from the next. I looked so forward to it coming so much that eventually, I asked Cassie if I could start volunteering two days each week.

She enthusiastically agreed. Looking at a calendar together, we found the days that were most needed for volunteer help and decided on Tuesdays and Thursdays.

Those rapidly became my favorite days of the week. I learned, before long, all the names of the elephant staff. There was Meghan, Matt, Michelle (an intern turned apprentice), Mara, Savannah, Shelby, and, of course, team lead, Cassie. They were all nice, and all very different. But they all shared the same passion—the elephants.

That, of course, was the best part of it all. Getting to know the elephants. The family.

There was Lungile, the non-blood-related "Aunt"; Semba, the mother; Punga, the oldest son; Sundzu, the middle boy; and Nandi, the brand-new baby girl. They were quite the family; they all had such personalities, as different as people.

Lungile, who was around twenty-six years old, was not blood-related to the rest of the family. She looked older than her years. I learned that she had suffered from health problems related to reproductive issues and had come close to death at one point. She was permanently on birth control so she could never bear young. I suspect this is what made her such a great aunt to Semba's children. Elephants are so much like people—she likely took joy in interacting with the little ones as she didn't have her own.

Behind the scenes, she was always getting her blood drawn, and eye drops put in her eyes. It felt like something was always just a little bit wrong. During their trainings, the keepers performed "stranger" practice with Lungile. They did this practice with her more than any of the other elephants because she had frequent vet examinations and often got shots, so it became very important for her to know that not all human contact was going to be uncomfortable or scary.

During this practice, one or more people would walk slowly up to Lungile, who would be pressed against the bars, and touch her. The first time I got to join in on this activity I loved it. Rubbing her and touching her rough skin, I couldn't help but feel a bit sorry for her. In the big picture, though, it was impossible to miss that she was overall simply happy to have a family to call her own.

She was loved by her elephant family, blood or no blood. She obviously loved them. I feel like I connected most with her. She was a tough girl who had been through a lot, and she continued to go through a lot. I was always taken by how well she endured it all, in good spirit no less.

Then there was Semba, the mommy, about the same age as Lungile. They were both rescued from Africa after their parents were poached. Both Semba and Lungile felt like sisters, from an outsider's perspective. They lost their parents and likely had a difficult beginning. However, they pulled through and were able to keep each other as family. Family isn't always about blood. I admired those two.

Especially Semba. She was always very protective of her young when I met her. She seemed like a strong mother, perhaps driven by her own experience of being motherless. Elephants have strong family values, so much more like humans than people realize. She was always a good mom—keeping her little one close, watching her play. At times she played with her boys, too. Also, like any mother, she seemed exhausted—standing still as her baby girl ran around her or suckled at her breast, simply wanting a breather.

She was a beautiful mother.

Next in the family was Punga, the oldest brother. He was quite the growing bull. Almost the size of his mother at just over age ten, he was masculine in his movements and a sight to see even at his age. He was quite like a teenage boy—one minute, he'd be playing around in the muddy water with his brother, Sundzu, the next he was going into musth early, like a full-grown bull ready to breed.

Musth is something bulls go through when they were looking for a female elephant to breed with. They become enraged with hormones, showing off in masculine ways, while the glands near their eyes weep profusely. During times of musth, bulls can often be dangerous, especially to smaller elephants. When charging toward females in an effort to breed, an unaware adolescent elephant could get caught in the path and harmed by the bigger bull.

This, of course, never happened at the zoo. Naturally, other female elephants, like Lungile, would protectively herd Nandi. And, if necessary, the keepers separated the musthing elephant.

Punga was destined to be a beautiful bull when he grew up.

Next in line was Sundzu. He was a few years younger than his bigger brother, Punga, and smaller, as well. He seemed to have quite a bit of spunk, though, being right between childlike and adolescent-like. He was always playing with his big brother and seemed to enjoy it, but at times he was noncompliant during trainings and other commands.

He, too, would grow up to be quite a large and beautiful bull.

Last, but most certainly not least, was Nandi. I remember seeing her before I even started volunteering. When she was first born, just a tiny little calf, unsure, scared, staying very close to mom. She was always hiding behind Semba or running around with her ears splayed out wide, spraying water at people, running full tilt toward nothing in the awkward and adorable way of a young elephant. Although she did a really good job during trainings, she was rather impatient and had a very short attention span. It was all around adorable. She was pretty much like any nearly three-year-old.

⚭ ⚭ ⚭

I loved volunteering. I loved the sunshine, I loved the workout, I loved the elephants, I loved learning. I was reading a lot about different issues involving elephants. I often asked the zoo-keeping team as many questions as I could, and I always tried to do the best job I could while I was there.

I often thought, *I could do this for a living. I could love this.*

I even applied, early on, for an apprenticeship. As my degree is in criminology rather than zoology, I was pleased to find out that although I was not selected, I was the second choice. Things were going well.

In this short period of time it felt like an eternity but in a good way.

I slowly began to feel like I was fitting in. I really, truly believed I could build a future here, whether I was ever hired on full-time or not. I wanted to be at the zoo, next to these elephants. Learning about them and finding new ways I could make a difference there. Discovering, too, how I could make a difference for elephants around the world. I had found something I was truly passionate about. It made sense to me. I couldn't think of anything that could keep me from them. I had found my place.

)( )( )(

Until mid-March, that was. I had been with the zoo only a month and a half, it seemed like no time at all, in hind-sight. But it was all about to come to a sudden halt. I began having pain, familiar pain. It just wasn't going away.

"Something is wrong, Nick," I told my husband.

However, I'd had pain so many times over my whole life similar to this, so it was hard to know. Plus, I had been to the hospital so many times that the idea of going again sounded terrible. But as the evening wore on, the pain was not letting up. It didn't matter how many Aleves I took, or how many hot baths I sat in. My abdomen was killing me.

We went to the hospital and waited in the waiting room. I'm not even sure how long—it always feels like forever in the ER waiting room. It was a typical scenario I know all too well. After a while, they take you back to triage. Then you go back to wait. Then, what feels like a year passes. Finally, they call you back to, hopefully, a room within which you wait for what seems like another year to see a doctor.

Unusually, we ended up in a private room. The usual cadre of nurses came and went. I remember an older female nurse who was very sweet, but who couldn't get my IV in. I ended up bleeding all over her hands and she wasn't even wearing gloves! That must have been some sort of hospital safety violation, but she seemed pretty old school about it. She just washed her hands and went about her day.

As we waited for the next thing—the next nurse visit, a scan, whatever was to come—we watched TV. *How It's Made* was on, endless twenty-minute episodes about how everything was made, from high-precision cutting machines to potato soup. Finally, after being sent out for an abdominal CT scan, the ER doctor came to see me. She was confident; spoke quickly but clearly, yet also had a very kind demeanor. I remember liking her.

"The CT shows you have a mass in your abdomen, on the left side. We're going to admit you," she told me with a sympathetic smile.

A short while later I was transported to a hospital room. It was in the new women's ward at TMC. Wow! That was the best hospital room I have ever laid eyes on, to this day. It was huge, bigger than a studio apartment in some cities. It was perfectly clean. My hospital bed was situated in the middle of it, surrounded by a folding couch that my husband could sleep on, a TV/DVD player combo, large wardrobes and drawers, a desk built into the wall, and a small fridge and microwave!

It was late, past midnight at that point. Nick got as comfortable as he could on the couch. I spent the night in fits of sleep as nurses came in to check my vitals, change out my IV fluid bags, and administer pain medication. I was told I could expect to see the doctor sometime that morning to talk about the plan and next steps.

It turns out, I got a really great doctor. He was kind, spoke slowly and clearly, and was patient with our questions. He sent me for a scan. The scan showed that my left ovary had ruptured due to a cyst and I had internal bleeding. I couldn't believe it!

I was lucky this time, though. All the scar tissue inside my belly from my last big surgery had created random pockets and one of those pockets held in the blood seeping out of my ovary. The blood filled that pocket and clotted, stopping the bleeding. Nevertheless, I had to have surgery to correct the issue.

The doctor decided to do laparoscopic surgery. I was thrilled by this because he said it would be only a few minor incisions. This was music to my ears compared to my 2014 surgery. Not much recovery time, he said.

He said he would schedule me for later that day. The time came, and he showed up to explain to me that we had been bumped by emergency surgery. I was feeling frustrated, largely because I hadn't eaten, and it was now day two. I understood, nonetheless. He said we would try again for the next morning.

The next morning came, and he showed up early to say that again there had been an issue and that he could not move forward with the surgery. Something about the robot he planned to use to assist wasn't working, and the only other one in the hospital was booked all day.

He said I could have some liquids in the meantime, while he worked to schedule the surgery again. However, as anyone knows, liquids don't suffice when you are hungry. It was day three by then, and I was in and out of pain, in and out of consciousness, thanks to the pain meds, and quite starving. I started to get emotional.

In particular, the hunger became the driving force in my mind. My pain was being managed well, for the most part, but I couldn't stand the emptiness. My brain couldn't understand it either. It began to fantasize. My husband recounted to me, later, that I was lying in bed and, unprompted, naming foods out loud that must have sounded good.

"Hamburger. Mmmm," I mumbled.

Or I'd look at him and smile, and say, "Grilled chicken."

And, if you're from Tucson, it comes as no surprise that I whimpered, "Eegee's."

Finally, late on day four, I was taken into surgery. From what I understand, it was a long one. Nearly three hours. However, from the doctor's report to my husband right afterward, and the pictures of my insides that he showed him, everything went well.

When I came out and regained consciousness, I was in a lot of pain. A lot more than I expected to be, I suppose. Once I was out of recovery and brought back to my room the doctor came to see me. He explained to both my husband and me that he had to remove my left fallopian tube and a giant blood clot (which, by the shape he made with his hands, was grapefruit-sized), but in order to do all of that he had to cut through and remove a ton of scar tissue. He said my abdomen and intestines were riddled with scar tissue and that I may feel tender because of that.

All I knew was that I felt tired. Having to recover again was going to be a chore. Standard recovery from abdominal surgery is four weeks, or even six, and I knew this was going to prevent me from going back to the zoo for a while. I began thinking to myself, *How likely is it for someone to have both of their ovaries rupture due to a cyst when they don't have any kind of cystic disease?* It made me start thinking about my overall health. I thought it was strange that now both ovaries had ruptured, not to mention that in the past (in 2008 to be exact) I had to have a hysterectomy due to severe endometriosis and rapidly growing fibroid tumors.

My mind was also on the zoo. I knew it would affect me, not being able to go back to the zoo right away, and that this would put a dent in the mental health work I had been doing with Dr. George. I thought, *What do I do next?*

All of these things combined made me think of an even bigger picture of my health—my future—*What's next?* I started thinking about family history. Cancer. I'd had ovary issues my whole life. Cysts had ruptured from my early twenties on. I was just "lucky" that internal bleeding only occurred these two times. In addition, I'd had a mass removed from my left breast in 2015.

This made me think of something my gynecologist had been pushing for–something he had mentioned to me several times–being tested for the cancer gene. More specifically, the Breast Cancer 1 and 2 genes, better known as BRCA.

CHAPTER 8

THE ELEPHANT IN THE ROOM

Right on cue, the four weeks passed, and I had healed. During this healing time, I made a decision. Having the second ovary rupture made me decide that I wanted, needed, to have the **BRCA** test done. I'd had too many female problems and came from a long line of female cancer carriers. I was trying to start my life over, and I would be damned if something like cancer was going to stop me from doing that. I wanted to get ahead of the game. I wanted to take charge of my physical health much like I was taking charge of my mental health.

I returned to the zoo in late April and picked up where I left off. It was wonderful to be back spending time with the elephants, watching them interact, touching their rough hide during stranger danger. Seeing Semba love on Nandi and watching Lungile watch over the youngsters with love. When I was there, I found that my mind was not plagued by worry or anything negative for that matter.

As far as the team goes, I was happy that they were so happy to take me back. Sometimes having setbacks like that makes it seem like you're not reliable, and that was my big concern. It was a little tough, after the surgery, but I pushed through. I found myself doing fine with the usual elephant crew tasks.

I had an appointment scheduled with the local university to get my gene testing done. I told Cassie, that I was going to be doing this. It felt very strategic in my mind.

As the next apprentice opening was a year away, if my test came back positive, I could do what I needed to do, recover, come back, put in a few more months and then apply again. It made total sense to me.

All of my zoo coworkers were curious. There were a lot of questions.

"Did you have cancer? Is that why you had this last surgery?"

"Do you have a mass somewhere now? Is that why you're getting tested?"

"If it comes back yes, you're going to be getting a mastectomy? Why do you think that's necessary?"

They were sweet when they asked these things. They were genuinely curious, and a little concerned. I explained to them, one, my own personal medical history to date and, two, the history of cancer within my maternal side and, three, how early the onset of cancer in my family tended to be. That most women in my family had cancer diagnosed by age forty, just a few years away for me. These were the reasons I thought it was important to know and to be proactive.

These were the best answers I could give. I didn't know much at the time; just that you needed to qualify in terms of medical and family history, and go through a counseling session. I would know more after my first appointment.

After being back for a little while, I felt like I was in the groove again physically and back up-to-date with all that had happened with the elephants and the crew. Right where I felt like I should be.

A few weeks later I met with one of the university's genetics counselors. There was a ninety-minute interview to make sure I qualified for the test. Who in my family had had cancer? What kind of cancer? What was their relation to me? What sorts of medical problems had I had? What was my lifestyle? It went on and on.

At the end of it all, I was told I qualified. The counselor could, to my surprise, take the blood sample then and there. She walked me down a hallway carrying a box—a special box that she alone was allowed to have control of. Inside was a vial.

She walked me to the phlebotomist. The counselor opened the box, took the numbers on the vial and wrote up a label. My blood was drawn, the vial was handed back to the counselor, and it was put safely away in the box. She personally resealed it and, I presumed, sent it off for testing.

I'm not sure how much time went by, but it seemed like a week at the longest before the genetic counselor called me with my results. She explained that I was positive for BRCA1 and that she wanted to schedule another appointment so she could explain to me, in detail, what that meant to me and what my options were.

I suppose, originally, I thought to myself that if I was positive, I would take care of it all and move on. It seemed like a task to get out of the way. At that moment, though, when I was told the results, I felt scared. Ninety percent of me knew, deep down, that the results were going to be positive, but when it came out of her mouth over the phone, I couldn't believe it. It was the strangest feeling, being told you are going to get cancer.

We scheduled a meeting, and when the day came, she ran through so much information. There were packets of info to take home afterward. I remember that we talked a lot about statistics—my likelihood of getting cancer compared to the rest of the population. It was pointed out that while the typical woman has an eight percent chance of getting breast cancer by age seventy, I had an eighty-seven percent chance—nearly a guarantee—and while less than one percent of women get ovarian cancer in their lifetime, the odds were that two in every three BRCA1 carriers would.

We also talked about how much of an impact family history and the onset of cancer in family members played a part in the timing of my likely cancer onset. In my case, members of my family had these cancers at young ages.

She explained a variety of surgical options—mastectomy without reconstruction, with reconstruction, nipple sparing vs. non-nipple sparing, implants, fat grafting, and on and on.

)( )( )(

After our meeting, my first step was to meet with the breast oncologist. I knew, in my head, what I wanted—nipple-sparing mastectomy with reconstruction. However, I was told I may not have options. Thankfully, as I soon learned, the oncologist at the university specialized in nipple-sparing procedures.

I also decided on implants, as deep inferior epigastric perforator flap (DIEP) breast reconstruction didn't make sense on someone with my petite frame and surgical history. They take chunks of fat living below the belly button and use it to reshape the breasts.

The breast oncologist said she wanted to get some pre-screening done before surgery just to make sure everything was clear and ready for surgery. Basically, she wanted to make sure I didn't already have cancer, which meant more blood work, a breast MRI and a mammogram. This was my second time in an imaging center wearing the open front, pink-tied, top only hospital gown specially made for women getting breast imaging and those who had breast cancer.

Going through the very uncomfortable mammogram—no woman on earth enjoys this—was even worse with small breasts like mine. Due to the fact that I have small breasts, it's not just that they are being crushed by this machine—the crushing pressure of it is excruciating for anyone going through the test—but the nurses are desperately yanking and pulling at your breast tissue and nipples trying to squish them into the machine so they are visible on the readout. Then, an awkward MRI where I lay facing down and my breasts went into these odd holes. Why both? It felt like the MRI should have been enough.

Box checked. Pre-testing completed.

ⅩⅩⅩ

A few days or a week later, I got a call from the breast oncologist's office letting me know I had a mass in my left breast. Just about a year earlier, I had a mass in my left breast—lower quadrant. It felt scary to hear that I had another one. The first was benign—could I be so lucky again? It made me feel, at that moment, that what I was doing had to be the right thing.

During the call, the nurse mentioned the doctor felt that, since the mass was in the upper/outer quadrant of the breast when the mastectomy was done she'd remove the lump and those lymph nodes altogether, if it was okay with me to get it all done at the same time.

Being a little nervous that this was my second lump and that I had already tested positive for BRCA, I said yes. Especially, since the nurse I was talking to said it may be cancerous. I was scared and wanted to get it all out. I wanted it over and done. Not to mention, the nurse was rather nonchalant about it–she made it sound like the easy answer.

My surgery was scheduled for July 12th. I felt like this gave me plenty of time–that I would have until July 12th to keep working with the elephants. Also, that I would recover in plenty of time for the next steps.

I felt nervous. It was early June at the time. My fear deepened. My original thought was to get it out of the way so I wouldn't have any more health concerns or issues. Now, though, I had a mass that could be cancer. It was overwhelming. Gloom and doom were starting to over-take me.

I couldn't help but fall into a bit of a pity party. It felt like my life was crashing down on me. I was trying to battle mental illness that was induced by my awful child-hood–lord knows at least the PTSD was. Neglectful, abu-sive mother; sex abuse; poverty; learning life the hard way; kids at a young age; struggling through school; ultimately choosing a career that blows up in my face. Now, at the same time, I was trying to battle health issues. The worst, at the time, was the 2014 health issue. I fell apart back then, and now I felt like it was happening again.

Unfortunately, I put up a façade. Not only did I have to tell people close to me that yes, I tested positive, now I also had to tell them I had a mass that could be cancerous. I did my damnedest to pretend it was no big deal like I was just rolling with the punches. However, Dr. George knew the real story. So did my husband. I was sick. They knew I was figuring that my luck was always bad, so how could this possibly turn out for the good? Of course, this recent seed of fear about the mass was probably stronger due to the positive BRCA test, but nevertheless, it was my reality.

What scared me most of all was that it might be cancer.

What would that do to my family? What was any of this doing to my husband? His mother died of breast cancer. That was one of the factors that lead to my decision to get the BRCA test done—to make sure that never happened to him again.

I had to schedule a follow-up after my ovarian surgery with my PA John. It was an insurance requirement, but he also liked to keep tabs on my health. Thank God the insurance required it, and thank God he had been with me for ten years and was no bullshit. He inquired about what was going on and what was next. I explained to him what had happened recently. He had already proactively read the report and made some light-hearted jokes about the coincidence of the other ovary rupturing. He explained to me that I needed to stay on top of my health; that I needed to be my own advocate.

Not long after uttering those words, we began to talk about the schedule—my first surgery, a double mastectomy, was happening in July, just a few weeks away. I told him that in the preliminary tests prior to the surgery they found a mass in my left breast—again.

I explained that the nurse had told me that since the lump was in the upper left quadrant of my breast that they planned to remove the lump, and the adjacent lymph nodes, during the surgery. All in one fell swoop. Convenient, right?

He flipped out!

"I can't believe these fucking doctors these days! It's just too easy to cut everything out, so you don't have to worry about it in the long run, rather than do some extra tests and talk to the patient about risks."

That was just the start of a rant about doctors and surgeons.

"Did they even talk to you about the risks that come with removing your lymph nodes?"

I responded that they hadn't—that I hadn't really thought about it. They made it seem routine.

"Did they even offer you a biopsy?"

I said that, in a sense, they'd offered it up, but said the easier option was removing it all at once.

"Of course, it's easier that way! Again, did they cover the risks?"

Again, I said no.

With a look of anger and disappointment on his face, he said there was a pretty solid chance I could get lymph-edema in my arm and that if the mass turned out to be benign, it would all be for nothing.

Lymphedema cannot be cured, only managed, he went on. He explained that it creates an excess of fluid in the limb area closest to it. It causes pain. The limb swells up to four times its normal size. The fluid can sometimes be drained, but it always comes back.

I cried in his office. I felt a little bit in over my head, and angry. Why hadn't they discussed the options or ad-vocated for me to do the biopsy? Why would they suggest, so flippantly, that I remove it all? When they explained that it was easier, I wondered who it was easier for?

He insisted that I made it happen, even if I pushed back the surgery date—that I get the biopsy done. If it wasn't cancerous, the lymph nodes must stay. I agreed.

He had helped me many times or provided medical in-sight. He was one of the few physicians I worked with who didn't sugarcoat things and who gave me the whole truth. I respected that in him. It is something I respect in people in general, but these days, especially in doctors.

※ ※ ※

I left his office and called the cancer center, telling them I had changed my mind. I told them I felt I had been ill-informed and wanted to get a biopsy before the surgery. I told them I did not want my lymph nodes removed for no reason; that I wouldn't risk lymphedema for nothing.

I very candidly asked the nurse I was speaking with why I was told over the phone, one, that I had a mass in my breast and, two, why wasn't I given options and risks for the procedures? She really couldn't answer. She just apologized, a lot.

A week and a half later I had my biopsy. They had rushed the request through, looking to avoid rescheduling surgery. It was a bit painful, but they got it, and they took quite a few chunks of it out of me. I was sore for a while, but nothing serious. Lo and behold, about a week later, the test results came back negative. It was a benign mass. Removing my lymph nodes would have been in vain.

I felt relief–it wasn't cancer. I wouldn't have to suffer from lymphedema. My mind was eased, just slightly–but I was still nervous about what was to come. At least at this point, though, I knew it was all still a preventative measure.

CHAPTER 9

MONSOON SEASON

It was the Fourth of July and I was so excited. We live in the foothills of Tucson, Arizona, which means we have views of at least four different spots down in the valley and one just up the hill from us that hold large public fireworks displays. It is so much fun watching the beautiful lights in the sky at night and hearing the crashing booms. It felt romantic any time my husband and I got to watch fireworks together.

But, most of all, the Fourth of July brought me excitement because that holiday marked the beginning of monsoon season. The black and grey skies would come. The lightning is beautiful. The rain comes down like it is trying to drown you. I've never seen, anywhere else, things bloom and turn green so fast after just a single rain. This would also be my first monsoon season working outside, at the zoo, in the elephant yard. I was both worried and excited for the challenges that would come with working there in the mud and the rain.

Nick and I both love the rain, whether drizzling, sprinkling, or pouring. But monsoon season is different. All day long it would be smoldering hot with bright blue skies—then, come evening, enormous, dark, foreboding clouds would race in and release massive downpours of rain that brought instant flooding, filling up dry riverbeds, making ponds of our backyards and turning streets into streams. Basically, for a few hours, Tucson was under water. By the next day, the summer sun would have dried the city, and the desert would be outrageously in bloom, but otherwise, it was like nothing had happened. That was until the evening came again. It's something you have to experience first-hand to understand. During monsoon season, Tucson, Arizona is spectacular.

In just under two weeks I would have my mastectomy done. It had been a busy couple of months since I had recovered from my surgery in March. Lots of hard work at the zoo. Today, though, was a national holiday, and for the first time in a while, I felt like I was on a little break. Monsoon hadn't come quite yet, but I knew it was close. It was in the air. At the moment I was enjoying the day, barbecuing, with my brother, husband, and boys. Typical barbeque day—hot dogs, chicken, burgers. The men were drinking beer. I had a Diet Coke, and the kids had some Sprite.

Holidays are cheat days, so we had plenty of snacks like chips and cookies. My husband had purchased fireworks. Most of the time he's pretty formal; well-spoken, and just an overall conservative person in his demeanor. However, one thing I love about him is how childlike he can become, especially if you get him around something that burns or explodes! He didn't just buy snakes and sparklers. He bought the biggest pack of the biggest fireworks he could find—legally—in Tucson. That night after dinner, we lit them all. They weren't the variety that shoots up into the air—instead, these splashed the ground with fountains of colors. Totally safe, and totally fun to watch.

We live on a cul-de-sac, so he assured me it would be safe and sane to set them off there. They were pretty tame fireworks, I guess, but still sparkly, loud, and fun! His favorite was the California Candles—handheld fountains that flowed sparks and colorful fire. He ended up dueling my brother with them. A scary moment, for me.

I went to bed happy that night. I felt great, it was a great day, and I was wiped.

ϟ ϟ ϟ

The next morning, I woke up not feeling awful, but not great either. My back kind of hurt and my stomach was a bit upset. Being no stranger to discomfort, I went about my day as I usually would. However, midday, I started having pain. Lots of cramping and some sharp shooting pain. Not like before with my ovaries. Higher, different.

I just tried to deal with it. Then I became nauseated. I ate something, hoping it would help it go away. Nope, it didn't. It made me feel full and gross. My thought was that perhaps it was something I ate the day before. I felt really bloated, with a lot of pressure building. I remember thinking that if I could just get something out–throw up or something–that I would feel better.

Despite the pain, I walked the dog that evening along with my husband. It seemed like it was not helping. Nothing was moving. Nothing was happening. Just the discomfort and pain.

I soaked in a hot bath that night. I told my husband I thought something was wrong; really wrong. At this point, he didn't totally take the sentiment lightly, but because the pain was different, we thought maybe I was just constipated or really bloated. We were unsure.

Then, however, finally, I got some relief. I threw up!

And didn't stop. It was like I threw up a bucket full of this really dark, green liquid. It was awful. It didn't smell like vomit. It smelled foul. I did feel a little better, though. The pressure was gone. I cleaned up, lay in bed, and was able to fall asleep for a little bit. But in the middle of the night, the same thing started again. I got up, in pain, and threw up like that again. It was starting to scare me. My stomach wasn't getting any smaller. I was still very bloated and it felt very solid. I was not passing any gas or using the bathroom either. Just throwing up, a lot.

With all the hospital visits I've had it was almost no big deal for me to go to the emergency room on my own. So in the morning, I told my husband to go to work. If they found anything wrong, I would simply let him know. He was hesitant but eventually agreed. I went to the local university hospital since that was where my mastectomy and all of my other surgeries were going to be done, and since that's where I saw Dr. George. I figured, for continuity of care, it made sense.

I went and waited. They asked all the typical questions. They pushed on my stomach, which, *surprise*, hurt. They asked if I had been throwing up. I told them about it, but I didn't throw up at the hospital so they decided to do a CT scan.

Meanwhile, while I was waiting on the results, they gave me some morphine for the persistent pain. By the time I got the results I hadn't had any morphine in quite some time, and the pain was creeping back in. The results, according to them, were negative. Everything appeared normal. They couldn't tell me why I was having pain or why I was vomiting, and just like that they gave me paperwork and kicked me out. "Try a bland diet" was their only advice.

Nothing had changed, though. I hadn't thrown up, but I also hadn't eaten anything. I drove home in pain. I called my husband, in tears. I felt like I was crazy. I had all this pain, yet they told me there was nothing wrong! The pain did not go away, so I decided I wanted a second opinion. That night, I talked to my husband, and we decided to go to Tucson Medical Center.

I went and I waited. They triaged me and had concerns. The only reason I think they admitted me was because I started vomiting at the hospital. Not to mention that I wasn't passing gas and I hadn't had a bowel movement in a few days. The ER doctor that saw me was baffled that I had been discharged by the university hospital. He said there was obviously something wrong, and that I needed to be admitted into the hospital for observation.

A short time later I got a room, and it began.

They gave me pain meds, which helped. They hooked me up to fluids and started pumping me full of laxatives. It was awful. I didn't want to swallow a single thing. I knew it would just trigger vomiting. However, the hospital doctor was sure I was just constipated. The problem was that at this point, anything I swallowed—water, pills—would induce intense vomiting of this greenish-brown liquid. But the doctor kept coming back to check on me, with no new ideas and kept throwing laxatives at me.

It was an awful day at the hospital. The night was terrible too. At one point I threw up two liters of fluid at once. The nurses seemed concerned. So, on the second day, a few things happened. They started giving me enemas and decided it was time to insert an NG tube down my nose and into my stomach. It all seemed to go by so fast during my first twenty-four hours there.

They explained that the tube would keep me from vomiting by suctioning out anything before it had a chance to build up. I don't know if any of you have had an NG tube, but it is terrible. They shove it down your nose, all lubed up with lidocaine gel, and I don't know if there is one, but it sure felt they needed to break through a membrane during the process.

The tube resisted going down, then I felt this horrible *POP*, followed by lots of pain as it slid down. You're supposed to try and swallow as it passes through your throat down to your esophagus. It's such an unnatural feeling, and it doesn't help that this is not a tiny tube. It was rather big, and in any case, it is a foreign object the body wants to reject.

Within an hour of it going in I had a sore throat, so they brought cough drops. I wasn't even allowed to drink water. The tube was connected to a suction container that could hold a maximum of 500ml. At the start, it filled up every day. The first 24 hours of having the tube in seemed like an eternity of discomfort between the stomach pain, the irritation, and discomfort from the tube, and not being able to find relief for my bloating. I was starving and so very thirsty. They were still pumping me full of fluids from the IV, and they were still forcing enemas on me, which were not working. Regardless, it made me feel like I had to get up and go to the bathroom. It was absolutely awful. As if I wasn't in enough discomfort, now I had this awful urge to go without the ability to do so.

Every single time I got up with the urge to go to the restroom a nurse would come in and disconnect the NG tube that was dripping with nasty, tar-like fluid from my insides. The tube would leak fluid onto my dressing gown, thanks to the callous carelessness of the nurses. Sometimes it leaked all over my bed. Maybe they were used to people's excretions and fluids, but personally, I felt disgusting.

Time passed so slowly. The doctors literally came in just once a day, and they'd all ask the same questions.

"Have you passed gas yet?"

It became a joke between my husband and me, as that was always the first thing they'd ask. Then they'd poke my stomach, sometimes listen to it, write something in a chart and then leave. The primary doctor, who I distinguished from the rest by his ability to prescribe meds, would come in, talk about laxatives and enemas, and shrug his shoulders. At this point it had been three days—I was exhausted, starving, angry, and feeling hopeless.

I needed to talk to Dr. George. I emailed him to let him know what was going on and told him my frustrations. I cried as I wrote the email. Without much delay, he called me. We discussed what was happening medically, what my symptoms were, what the doctors had or had not done so far. He said that in his opinion, it sounded like some sort of severe ulcer or upper bowel obstruction or an obstruction in general. He asked if I had been seen by a surgeon yet. No, I replied in tears. He recommended that I talk to the doctor about a consultation and see where that got me. I agreed that it sounded like a good idea and that his thoughts on the cause made sense.

I talked to my husband about it after the conversation with Dr. George. He agreed, and so when our nurse came in, we discussed the issue with her. We asked her why we hadn't seen a surgeon. She agreed that she was thinking it might be a bowel obstruction. She said the doctor wasn't there anymore, as it was evening, but she would reach out to the surgeon on call to get a consultation.

⚒ ⚒ ⚒

Now four long days into my stay, I was at the end of my rope. I lay in bed that night after Nick had gone home, medicated and tired from a day that was a repeat of the last several. Vomiting, laxatives, pain, consoling nurses, useless doctors. As my mind drifted in that dark hospital room, for once quiet except for the odd noises of the machines connected to my IV lines, I thought of the elephants at the zoo. Those thoughts carried over into a dream.

I stood in an open field, a summer sun beating down, warming first my flesh, then my core. I was alone and wondering where I was. Then, from around a rock precipice a few hundred yards away, a family of elephants appeared one by one.

Once several came into view, including one that was toddler age, I realized this was my family of elephants!

Looking around again, it occurred to me that I was standing in the wide-open field of the Reid Park Zoo elephant exhibit. It was different, though, so I hadn't recognized it. But now, seeing the elephants walking toward me, I realized all the barriers were gone. No fences, no giant steel gates, no locks. Everything else was the same, but I was now free to be amongst the elephants.

I couldn't restrain myself. I ran toward them. Tears of joy ran down my cheeks and flicked back over my shoulders in the headlong breeze I ran into. They trumpeted together as if to greet me. Suddenly I found myself in the middle of the herd. The elephants stood around me, looking upon me with a mix of happiness and worry in their eyes. They gently touched me with their trunks, agitated. Nandi stepped toward me and reached out her trunk, hugging my waist.

This behavior reminded me of nature documentaries I had seen before. Elephants, such social creatures, worry about their family members when they are ill and will try to comfort them. I knew, then, that this is what my elephant family was doing.

I woke with a start. A nurse was standing over me. "Honey, it's time to take your vitals."

"What time is it?" I murmured.

"It's about 2 a.m., dear. Once I'm finished, you can go back to sleep."

And I did, but my rest remained dreamless the remainder of the night. I woke to a day of activity.

The surgeon responded in record time. He and a team of lackeys rolled into the hospital room like a taskforce that morning. They took over the room. He ordered another CT scan since the hospital doctor had simply referenced the one from the previous hospital visit from earlier in the week at the university. The surgeon was baffled by this. He wanted to get his own imaging done.

He returned to my room after the results were read and said quite plainly that it was a bowel obstruction. He remarked that he didn't understand the holdup. There was no reason it should have taken four days to get him involved. He committed to going in, finding out what the problem was, and fixing it. He mentioned there were some risks involved that arose from the delay. He also explained that due to the delay he was not going to wait–he was going to perform the surgery that night.

Disappointed that I was slated for another surgery, I was also relieved that the puzzle had been solved. I also knew that there was simply no way I was going to be having my mastectomy, scheduled for just one week from then. It was going to be pushed back. Not that I was giddy about getting the mastectomy; it's just that I had a plan to get it done as soon as possible so I could get back to the zoo, back to the elephants. I wanted to have a few months back at the zoo before the next apprenticeship was up for grabs.

It felt like everything was derailing.

I asked the surgeon if that meant the NG tube could come out. He gave me the bad news—the answer was no. He explained that due to the delay, there would be some serious paralysis of the bowels and that if I tried to eat or drink anything, it would all still come back up. It was going to take time for my bowels to wake back up.

With that, I was prepped and taken into surgery around 9 p.m. that night.

※ ※ ※

When I woke up, two things were very apparent to me—first, the NG was definitely still there as promised and, second, they had cut me again on the same scar from my 2014 surgery, not quite sternum to pubic bone like before, but almost.

I was in a lot of pain. There was still no relief from the discomfort. I felt extremely sick. However, the doctor visited and said that everything went really well. It was the massive amount of scar tissue binding up in my bowels that had caused the obstruction, very likely due to the multiple abdominal surgeries I had been through, and that it was not unlikely that I might have another such obstruction someday, but that this time no permanent damage had been done internally. He said they had performed a treatment—putting in some kind of mesh during the surgery to help prevent obstructions in that area again.

When I woke up next, it was around midnight on day six. I didn't know how much longer I'd have to be there. They told me it was time to get up and start walking around–this was, from what I was told, again and again, the best way to wake up the bowels. The problem was, I was in a ton of pain. Not only that, I felt humiliated. I had to carry around this nasty clear tube that was stained green, up my nose, taped in place for everyone in the hospital hallways to see as I dragged around my IV stand.

I felt like a leper.

It was a struggle to walk, but I never stopped trying. I thought if I could just make it far enough to see out the hospital windows into one of the nicely planted courtyards, I would be happy. It was sunny during the day, and breezy, with clouds building more each time I walked by. I wished I could be out there.

Part of my recovery included a new set of doctors, along with the old set of doctors, rotating into my room. My surgeon, who seemed very experienced and straightforward, but friendly, rarely came around. He was quite obviously a very busy man. However, all his resident lackeys, a team of about five people, with head lackey being a very cocky over-the-top jerk, came by regularly.

He'd come in and complain about my NG tube being connected wrong, or whatever, and never stopped complaining that the nurses didn't know what they were doing. However, the nurses would come in later and complain that what he did made it harder to do one thing or another—most of the time, I was a bit lost as to what they were talking about.

At this point I was spending entire days, mostly alone. It had been over a week; my husband was coming in the evenings, sometimes in the mornings, but I told him to go back to work because I would need him around when we went home—when I was discharged. I explained there was nowhere for him to be overnight and that it was useless for both of us to lie around and stare at crappy TV or the blank wall.

When no one was there, I also felt less obligated to be awake, which was nice. Nick was always telling me that I should sleep if I was feeling tired, but I just couldn't when he was there. I felt like I had to be awake—to be social— probably because we were spending so much time apart.

One of my best friends, Danielle, had already pur- chased a plane ticket to come into town from Oregon to be with me the week leading up to my mastectomy. In- stead, however, she was going to show up, fingers crossed, right as I was being discharged from the hospital after this surgery. We had been texting on and off. She was baffled. She simply couldn't believe that another random emer- gency situation had happened to me. To be completely honest, I couldn't believe it either. Do I not have the worst luck in the world?

✖ ✖ ✖

My husband was there visiting me after work one day–not quite sure what day it was, as by then I had lost most of my sense of time–and he said it was sprinkling outside. The rain had arrived; the monsoon had now officially started. I thought to myself, *That's great, I have these big windows where I can look out into the pretty courtyard and watch it rain.* We talked and visited for a while, and as we did, the skies were growing greyer and the wind was blowing harder. But it was getting dark, and Nick was getting tired. With nowhere to sleep in my hospital room, he departed.

Just a little while after he left it was completely dark outside, and I could just barely hear the rain on the roof. The windows were thick and did not open. I couldn't see the rain falling because there were no lights in the courtyard. Worst of all, I couldn't smell it. When it rains in the desert, it smells clean. At first, like wet dirt, but after a while, the trees and plants come alive. They smell very different than the mossy, piney smell of, say, Flagstaff. The smell that comes through is the most wonderful aroma of what I call the "rain bush." My husband once told me what it was called, but I can never remember.

My only chance to see the rain was every once in a while when lightning streaked across the sky. During monsoon, lightning is intense. When it streaks across the sky, it lights up everything like someone suddenly turned on a bright LED light for a split second. When that happened, I'd get a glimpse of the trees moving in the wind, and of raindrops falling from the sky. Because the storm was right overhead, the thunder was almost instantaneous. It had been cloudy and rained on and off a few times prior to this, but tonight's storm was different. This was the big one. During monsoon season there is always at least one big storm. It could last a few hours, a whole day, or even a few days. But there was always one big one. This was the one.

As the night wore on the storm got bigger, bolder. And much louder. Eventually, I could hear every gust of wind, every raindrop, and I could see the non-stop light show it brought. The nurses were getting frightened that the power might go out, or something else would happen. That is understandable, from their point of view. However, it soothed me, and I was peaceful.

However, my husband was not peaceful.

While I was at the hospital, stopped up and finding momentary peace in this storm, my husband was at home battling our house which had decided to back up the pipes into our shower. It was a large, step-down shower, and that night sewage backed up into the shower and would not drain. This problem continued for a few days. Oddly, it was the worst the night of the big storm. My husband later told me that he thought the house was sympathizing with me and wanted me home.

During the days after my surgery, the fluid the NG tube pumped out slowly reduced. The surgeon decided, eventually, that it was okay to take it out. I was so happy. He also decided I could begin a liquids diet, as a start; sort of as a test run to see if things stayed down. At this point I was okay with that–I was honestly scared to eat. Not only was I severely nauseated, but I'd just had surgery. I knew if I threw up it was going to hurt like hell, and I also knew they would shove that NG tube back in.

However, to my surprise, everything stayed down!

I was on the liquids diet for twenty-four hours. Then, I was on a soft foods diet. Mashed potatoes, ice cream, things like that. I could barely eat though since I hadn't in such a long time. After surgery, I was hooked up to a TPN–a weird pack of fluid that was full of minerals and vitamins–and a lipid IV for fats. It didn't stop my body from depleting itself, though.

They put me back on stool softeners, laxatives, and enemas. I wasn't allowed to leave until I had a bowel movement. Since I hadn't had one now in probably twelve days, it felt like this would be the end of me. But then it arrived. It was the same day Danielle arrived, and guess what; I was still in the hospital. She wasn't supposed to be there, though, until the middle of the day. Three-ish that afternoon, I think. But it was exciting that my bowels were finally working.

By the time Danielle was picked up at the airport by my husband and brought directly back to the hospital, a discharge plan was being put into place. I was happy to be leaving, happy she was there, and happy to be going home. I would finally get to sleep in the same bed as my husband, which I now hadn't done for two weeks. That is how long I ended up in the hospital–two fucking weeks.

It was cloudy the day we left–just a little sprinkle of misty rain. It did rain again after I left the hospital, quite a few times. However, my favorite part of the monsoon, the bulk of it, the hurricane-like storms that roll in and take over each July, the part when you can lie in bed and watch in awe, I had missed. It all happened while I was in the hospital. The monsoons in Tucson that year, in 2017, were record-breaking. I had no idea 2017 was going to be a record-breaker for everything, though. In my rainy-day world, the streak had only just begun . . . again.

CHAPTER 10

NO RETURN

The bowel obstruction had done a number on me in many ways. I lay in bed for two weeks straight, not eating, in pain, on drugs. My body deteriorated. Sure, I lost some fat–great. However, I lost lots of muscle mass too, as well as strength and endurance. I also lost a little of my fire while I was there. In certain moments, of course, I was down on myself and on the world, but I've always picked myself up and kicked myself in my own ass and moved forward.

This time was different.

These thoughts were rolling through my head. I lost my uterus when I was so young. I suffered so much pain over the years with female health complications. I almost died in 2014 and lost another piece of myself, physically, and my life, career, and sanity. I found a prospect in the elephants, and I had that rug pulled out from under me in

March. Then, it was pulled out again with the obstruction in July.

Knowing that I was BRCA positive and having a mastectomy scheduled–or, at this point, rescheduled to September–I knew I was not going back to the zoo anytime soon, much less going back to normalcy, for a long while.

This broke my heart.

I have been a go-getter for as long as I can remember. I rose from a life of poverty and ignorance; of torture and hate to become educated and successful. I was active in my community, and I had developed strong convictions. My life choices had taken me from ghettos to government.

But it wasn't enough, apparently. Life stepped in and destroyed all that. Losing the elephants, something I had loved my whole life, and the path I had just found that could have had a future–all gone. *Taken*, I thought.

I was so very determined about applying for the next apprenticeship in February. Without a degree that fit the job, I knew I needed experience. Minimum, they wanted you to have a bachelor's–which I did–despite it being unrelated. They also wanted people with experience, something I would have gained from my volunteer work there. I had been reading about elephants. Studying them. I'd learned about their biology, their habitats, the different ways they were being threatened by human encroachment. I was researching conservation efforts and zoo practices. Coupled with my volunteer work, I thought that in the coming year, February 2018, I could apply for an apprenticeship and damn it, I would get it.

Plainly, that plan had been foiled.

Originally, I was on the fast track through the BRCA process. Mastectomy in July, reconstruction in August, radical hysterectomy by October. I would be back by November or perhaps December, giving me a few more months to work there, learn more, get better before my next interview.

Not happening.

Thanks to everything that had transpired during the monsoon season, my mastectomy was instead going to be in the fall. That meant reconstruction wouldn't happen until November or December. Then, when it came to the final surgery, who knows—maybe January or February, but in any case, too late. Right on the nose of apprenticeship interviews.

All of that coupled with my physical inability at that point made me feel so lost. Hopeless. The pride I had found in rising up from the flames was taken, snuffed out. Now, there was only smoke. A hint of what was before.

Because everything happened so quickly and kept on happening after I started volunteering, I was also terrified.

What would the zoo think of me?

What would the keepers wonder?

"Is she a drama queen? Unreliable? More trouble than she's worth?"

Had I found what I always wanted, without expecting it, only for it to be destroyed by some sick twists of fate? It was a strange time for me, thinking about the zoo, which I did often. At that point, I was probably overthinking it. Maybe even obsessing a bit. No, I *was* obsessing. I wanted to work with the elephants so very badly. It was all I wanted anymore. I ended up having all of these terrible thoughts, wondering if that was even still a possibility.

Perhaps even worse, I found myself in an all-or-nothing mindset. If I couldn't return to the zoo as a volunteer and work with the elephants and keepers, then I felt like I didn't deserve to see them. If I wasn't earning my keep there, what made me special enough to be there at all? I felt like I hadn't earned the right for special treatment. Working with the elephants had been a huge investment of time, blood, sweat, and tears for everyone else on the team. I felt like I hadn't given enough of that, yet.

If I could even go back, would I make going back to the zoo awkward? Being the person I am, I'd been honest about everything with the keepers. Did that make it weird to go back? Would they accept me again, as they had before? Was I the same person to them?

Before all my surgeries, people had always told me I should write a book. It wasn't until the elephants gave me purpose again, something that was mine, something that I could do and love, something I could believe in, something I had perhaps lost before I even had it that made me truly think about telling my story, actually attempting a book, because then there would be a happy ending.

At home, after my obstruction surgery, I was compelled not just to tell my story, but to shout it! However, at the time, it was just a jumble of feelings, thoughts, desire—no action yet. I couldn't muster that. I was in much too dark a place. Even after feelings of wanting people to know what I had been through, what life was like, had bubbled up inside I doubted myself to the core. I thought to myself, *Who would want to hear my story? Who would even care? Why is it worth knowing?* Besides, I'm not the only one out there with a story to tell, so why would I have the gall actually to do it?

In a nutshell, this was my mental state.

My physical state at the time was far worse, believe it or not.

I was lying on mountains of therapeutic pillows, drowning in reruns on Netflix, suffering in pain and then an oxy haze when I couldn't avoid taking a pain pill. Due to the nature of the most recent surgery, food was weird for a while. I didn't really want to eat. I craved almost nothing. When I did eat, it tasted strange, like my senses had been short-circuited.

My digestive system failed to work properly. Sure, there was no more blockage, but now I was permanently taking laxatives and stool softeners. My bowels might as well have been in a coma. This meant drinking crazy amounts of water which left me feeling crampy, nauseous, bloated. Unhappy.

At some point; it finally hit me, I knew I was not the one in control. Life was. I had attempted to get ahead by getting tested for the BRCA gene mutation, then scheduling the surgeries to be proactive. But you can't stop the force of life. Regardless of my best-made plans, life still delivered great twists and turns and just plain dropped me somewhere I hadn't been before. I had no idea when I would return to the elephants and, at that point, I wasn't sure I ever would.

My next surgery wasn't scheduled until September. I had about a month and a half between the two surgeries, and I realized that wouldn't be very much time, that I would likely end up getting just healthy enough to feel normal before my double mastectomy. And I knew beyond that day that I wouldn't understand or even know what to expect normal to be. There were so many things going on in my head all at once: losing the elephants so quickly after finding them and feeling like maybe I had made a mistake by trying to stop something before it started. I was all over the place in my head–grateful that I had survived through multiple emergency surgeries, but also sad, dark.

I wondered why. And what did I do? What had I done to make all this bad stuff happen to me in my life? What was to become of my body after all this? How could I ever expect it to function correctly again to do such a difficult job like working with the elephants at the zoo? The brief time I had between surgeries, I often found myself discussing these huge fears and disappointments with Dr. George.

I was on a temporary roller coaster. Most of the time going down. But I did go up at times, reminding myself here and there that I had survived so many things. I tried to keep in mind that eventually, all of this would pass as well. This up-and-down roller coaster became my whole life during that time between surgeries. For better or worse, these feelings came and went with frequency until September.

CHAPTER 11

FATE OR FAKE

September arrived, and thoughts were piling up in my head. I had come to terms with the BRCA prophylactic surgeries before, prior to my emergency obstruction surgery. That very surgery, however, had derailed the timeline and now the lead-up to my next surgeries and my inability to work with the elephants had pushed me into a depression. I found myself going over the previous few months of doctor visits and counseling sessions with quite a bit of regret.

Scheduling the genetic testing at the local university was the first recurring thought. After March, when my second ovary ruptured, I had decided to take action. I was going to be in charge of my own health. No more leaving it up to fate. I thought if I was proactive, I could avoid what had happened to many of the women in my family–they had suffered from a number of female health problems, mostly female cancers, at a young age.

I thought back to how simple the counselor made it sound. How quick and easy the process was to be, and how there were so many choices. She had painted a picture of advances in medicine that made the whole process so much more focused on aesthetics than it had been before. As time grew closer to the first BRCA surgery, however, a lot of what she had discussed with me, a lot of what I thought would be options, really weren't ideal or even possible. Honestly, I felt a bit misled.

I was originally told by the genetic counselor that there was a myriad of options available to all patients. That they could do the double mastectomy and immediately put in implants; that they could put in expanders or even remove fat from my body to replace breast tissue. But when I met with the plastic surgeon later in the process but before my obstruction surgery, what it boiled down to was those options were not for me. Every patient is different, I learned, and what the counselor had told me was broad brush. He said, with certainty, that most of those options are very uncommon, and that the only option I had was having expanders inserted, which meant a longer recovery and a lengthier process before the reconstruction could occur. I felt so misled. As a matter of fact, most of the appointments had been full of disappointment. I was left with serious doubts about the process and the eventual outcome.

I was scared. Overwhelmed.

Through all those thoughts, I again began to feel the despair creeping in. I was making this choice, despite the future I hoped to have at the zoo. Perhaps it seems silly to weigh those two together—my health against working with animals. However, I don't know that I can describe the feelings that giving my time to be near to these elephants gave me.

The whole process I had found hope in for my life felt like it went from a well-laid plan to a disaster. Time, suddenly, felt like it was slipping away. It was time to go through with a double mastectomy and insertion of the expanders. I was so scared; I did not know what to expect at all. I mean, they told me exactly what to expect from their point of view, but they never seem to know what it's going to do to you, as a person, or what you're going to feel physically and mentally when it is all done.

The worst part about it all was that in my head, I knew this was my choice.

I know this thought should make me feel liberated, in charge of my future even! But instead, I was terrified at that moment and felt like I was making a huge mistake. I thought to myself that I had just spent the last six months getting through mental health hang-up, surgeries, healing and trying to get better. Then only to start another six months of healing and getting better while feeling sick and struggling to work on my body. Not only did I want to be physically able to return to my volunteering at the zoo eventually, but I desired to feel like a woman again on the outside—to have the figure I used to see in the mirror, what I felt like I lost in 2014, gained back, then had taken from me again.

As panicked as all this made me, I said nothing. I stuck to my original decision because logically it still made the most sense, and honestly, I didn't want to seem like I was indecisive. Lying in the hospital bed waiting for the surgeons to come in I just accepted where I was in that moment.

When the surgeons came in, they drew all over my chest and breasts with a marker, assuring me that everything was going to go wonderfully and that I had nothing to fear. The breast oncologist even made a joke

"When you're through all of this you're going to have a great rack!" she said with a smirk.

As if "that" was supposed to make it all better, or if it was even true. Plus, what was wrong with my current rack? (Other than the obvious genetic mutations).

Then, the anesthesiologist showed up. Everything actually felt better from that moment on as they gave me anti-anxiety medication before we headed to the operating room.

Thank God!

I've never seen so many doctors and surgeons in one place. It was quite the symphony of procedures about to take place—a double mastectomy with expanders put in place afterward. They were going in to make room for the reconstruction that would eventually happen. This meant two head surgeons, with at least two residents per surgeon, and a team of five nurses and techs along with an anesthesiologist and his two residents. It was quite the show. As flashes of light passed my eyes while they adjusted the overhead lights, I saw white and green swirling around the OR as they positioned themselves. Then a mask was placed over my face, and I heard the word "breathe," and just like that, all their chattering melted away.

It was surreal. I drifted like Alice in Wonderland; then I was out.

)(()(()(

I woke in the worst pain. I was so very stiff, and sore. I felt sick. I tried to move and get comfortable, but nothing worked. I felt anxious.

"Nick!" I called out.

The nurse came over and said he was out in the lobby.

"You can see him in a bit. You took longer than you should have to wake up."

I always hated that shit. Why make your spouse or parent wait? Why make the patient wait? Never made sense to me; I just needed my husband.

I told the nurse I was feeling sick. She gave me some crackers to calm my stomach, but I puked anyway.

Finally, they let Nick back. I cried when I saw him. I felt so depleted and so grateful to be alive in that moment. I'm not sure what it was; I had not come close to death in this surgery, but my body was telling me something. It was tired, weary, almost at its quitting point. I knew that this recovery, more than others, was going to be a rough one. But in that single moment, I just needed Nick. I needed him then more than ever.

Hardly any time had passed between this surgery and the last one. No real significant recuperation had happened mentally or physically, and here I was, right on schedule. Well, the newest schedule for my latest surgery. I didn't know it yet, but I was in mourning for my body, my life, my connection with my new husband, my connection with who I was and what was next.

They literally carved off my chest, but it felt more like my heart.

My hospital stay was only twenty-four hours. I told my husband to go home that I would be fine. Dr. George came to see me in the afternoon. He listened to me talk, did some aromatherapy, then he left, as well. I slept as much as I could before my release. What I looked like now didn't hit me until I got home.

At this point, I'd had three stomach surgeries and a double mastectomy. My stomach was carved up from pubic bone to sternum, and I had big healing incisions on my breasts now. Drains were coming out of both sides of my chest, and the two small tubes in my abdomen just above my belly button were nerve blockers. Thank God for those! I was still in so much pain. Plus, my body was still pretty out of shape from everything else. Long story short, I was discouraged.

I was surprised at how much pain I was in since I had nerve blockers. The surgeons prescribed oxycodone, but I had never taken just oxy before. After previous surgeries, I had Percocet, and the prescription was for thirty pills. But this time it was just 100 pills of oxy. I did not always take them every four to six hours as suggested–sometimes I held off and just took one a day. But I did take them every day, minimum. Then one day, I ran out. *No big deal.* It was nice to have the relief when I needed it, but obviously it was time to depend on just Aleve.

I had never experienced anything like that before but depending on Aleve did not work out. I didn't realize it right away, but my body had become used to pain relief through an opioid. I thought I was getting better, but once the oxy ran out, I was sweating, cramping, suffering from headaches, migraines, nausea. I thought I had the flu at first. The shakes, though, and the loss of appetite and lack of fever made me wonder.

My husband and I started considering–was my body addicted? That was a lot of pills. I had never taken that many before, for that long. I felt desperate at the moment. My follow-up appointment was still a ways away, and the only thing on my mind was that I just needed more to get me through. I had no idea what I was doing at that moment, thinking that more pills were the answer. I've never been one to take meds. I found an old prescription for pain meds and not realizing that they expired, tried to get it refilled to get me through until I could see a doctor. The pharmacist, of course, denied the refill.

I felt blindsided by all of this. I'd been through major surgery, so getting a strong pain medication like this didn't seem strange. Plus, the plastic surgeon's assistant pushed that he didn't like his patients to be in pain.

"Don't worry," she had said in an attempt to be reassuring, "he prescribes oxycodone because it works so well. As long as you're in pain when you're taking it, you can't get addicted."

Tell that to my body. I suppose because of this attitude, though, the doctors who were involved in my surgery didn't prep me for how to get away from using the pain meds. Nor did they make any kind of plan for helping me feel better after I ran out. Instead, I just hit the end of the road and fell off the cliff.

As my body was going through so much, and my thoughts were racing with anxiety and fear and panic, I called Dr. George for help. He prescribed me what he called "comfort meds," agreeing that it sounded like my body was going through some withdrawal. They included a mild anti-anxiety med, an anti-nausea med, something for cramping, and something to help with sleep.

None of them were narcotics. It turned out to be a miracle cocktail, as the symptoms were shortly all gone. When my mind cleared, and I realized what had happened, I felt scared and angry. Nobody had prepared me for what the medication could do—what it could lead to. When you are in a lot of pain and encouraged by your doctors to use the medication prescribed, you just take them. My body had acclimated to the pills, and then, just like that, they simply ended. No one is there for you. I can completely understand why people with injuries or chronic pain become addicts. Doctors just prescribe and hand over these powerful pills and don't discuss the risks; they don't cover how to get off the pills. They even suggest that you cannot get addicted if you are in legitimate pain. If I hadn't been able to look to Dr. George for help, I would have suffered alone.

Still recovering, with drains leading out of my chest and expanders in, it was finally my first follow-up appointment. One of the drains got to come out, as there was no more fluid build-up on the right side. The left drain had to stay in as there was still a lot of build-up on that side.

I explained to the plastic surgeon's assistant what had happened with the oxy. She furrowed her brow at me, acting like she was listening, but seemed to be in disbelief that I could find myself addicted. I asked her—for the next surgery—if it would be possible to have Percocet rather than straight oxy.

In a very condescending way, she asked, "Do you understand what Percocet is?"

I replied that, yes, I did, it was Tylenol with a smaller dose of oxy in each pill. She didn't seem to get it, so I just left it at that. I guess that first follow-up appointment gave me the big picture. The real picture of the process. I got one tube out, but one tube was left in, and they weren't even going to start filling the expanders yet. They didn't even really know when that part would begin. First, they had to make sure the drains were both out and that I was healing properly.

My mastectomy was done at the beginning of September, but they were projecting it would be around Christmas before the implants could be put in. I think it was probably that day, if not immediately after, that the big shadow of acceptance fell over me. I was not going to go back to the zoo in time for the next apprenticeship, and I didn't know when I would, if at all.

It wasn't just acceptance that fell over me. It was a complete realization that I was trying to control everything. My future, my body, my genetics, for Christ's sake! It occurred to me as I wound down the first part of the BRCA surgery process that absolutely nothing turned out the way I was told. The timeline was completely off. And, there were just too many variables—too many wrenches in the works that happened before it.

So, why should I continue to stress myself? I started to feel like I had to roll with what came next. And that is exactly what I did. I healed for a while, with both drains finally out now. They took the air out of my expanders and slowly began the fills. This would be a long process with frequent visits to the cancer center. They were projecting Christmas time for the implants to go in, replacing the expanders.

I did okay during this. I was hopeful. Once I let go of the control, all I could do was wait. And wait, I did.

CHAPTER 12

CHRISTMAS

September. October. November. This surgery seemed to take a unique toll. It felt like the cherry on top–the final thing that pushed me over the edge. I was tired, weak, and quite sore. My days were filled with resting, small exercises, and doctor visits. I continued my weekly visits with Dr. George and added into the mix were follow-ups and expander filling appointments. That troublesome left breast had its drain removed eventually. Fill, after fill, very slowly, with some touch-ups here and there, I reached 500CCs of fluid. I was done.

Well, not quite.

Once you are done with the fills, you have to let it settle and stretch the skin for a few weeks. There I was at the end of November, stretching and waiting. The implants were projected for December 6th. They would remove the expanders and, at long last, put in silicone! Typically, for aesthetic purposes, there is a fat-grafting process that goes along with this. They remove the expanders, put in the implants, and then take fat from somewhere on your abdomen via liposuction. They inject this fat all over your chest and around your breasts so that your breasts appear more natural. Like they would if you were a typical woman who gets breast implants for aesthetic purposes.

Of course, originally I was on board for this as I wanted to look as normal as possible. That was until I found out, late in the game, what the recovery process looked like. The procedure sounds simple on paper, but the liposuction causes extreme edema, bruising, swelling and has a high risk of infection. Not to mention you have to wear an abdominal binder to help reduce the swelling and keep everything in place. The total healing process can be up to three months long!

I thought to myself, *I've already been through so much healing, so much pain, so much waiting—is it really worth torturing myself for aesthetic purposes?* In the end, it was an easy answer for me—no. The plastic surgeon cautioned me that there could be visible ripples, dents, dimples, flexing of muscles without the fat injection over the implants. I heard him. Although he accepted my answer, because he had to, I don't think he heard me. The whole team found it bizarre. The surgeon even said he didn't think he'd ever done the reconstruction without fat grafting.

It occurred to me that the reconstruction was important for me to feel like I was still a desirable woman, but I simply wasn't willing to go to that extent for vanity. Not after what I'd been through already. I chose mental health first–physical health first.

I was doing my best to be well in both ways. I was discussing all the options and decisions I had been making with Dr. George, attempting to be mindful and realistic with my expectations surrounding the outcomes of this surgery. I was also trying to keep positive by getting out as often as I could for fresh air and doing some of the things I loved. A few times over the last few months after the worst had passed with my mastectomy recovery, Nick and I had gone to the zoo just to walk around and visit the elephants.

Nick and I had always enjoyed walking around the zoo, and I was excited to see the elephants. I had missed them so much! Watching them now, as a visitor, was so much different than it was back before I started volunteering. Before, I would stand and wonder who was who. I tried to catch glimpses of characteristics that matched the information on the signage. Not that it mattered so much back then, because I just enjoyed watching them. I could observe them forever.

Now, though, I felt connected. As they walked around or played, I could explain to Nick who was who, what their ages were, why they typically acted the way they did, and what I had come to love most about each.

At the same time, there was anxiety and worry when we visited. I was unsure about running into the elephant team. I guess it was because I felt like I had started strong and then, in some ways, failed. With that came a feeling of drama surrounding both the expected and unexpected surgeries. I had no idea what they thought of me; if they considered me unreliable or incapable.

During one of those trips, the last one that year, we did run into a couple of people on the elephant team. They were full of smiles and seemed happy to see me. That helped resolve some of the anxiety I was feeling.

Then it was December. My surgery was scheduled right on cue, on December 6th. I was quite excited, but not because of the surgery. Rather, I was excited that the surgery would be done and over, and I would have recovered in time to simply enjoy Christmas. This was looking to be my first happy month in a very long time, as I adore Christmas! It's my favorite time of year—all the thoughtfulness, food, and coming together as a family. Not to mention the twinkle lights! I also rather enjoy the challenge of finding the people I love that one thing that will light up their lives come Christmas morning. I just wanted to get on the cutting table and be done with it as soon as possible.

Like most people living in Tuscon, we had our fake, pre-lit tree we'd gotten in anticipation for Christmas that November. Nearly eight feet tall with one thousand bright white lights! I love that tree. It was already up. I put my tree up on Black Friday. We called it our "fancy tree."

Decorated in gold, silver, copper, and chocolate—the color, that is.

It was set up in our living room. I was counting the days, though, as we got closer to Christmas until we could go out and get a fresh-cut pine tree to put in the dining room. That's the one we call the "family tree." We adorn it with old memorable ornaments, fun Star Wars ornaments, ugly but meaningful ornaments, and colorful string lights.

I was ready for the surgery to be done. The day arrived. The surgeon said it would only take about an hour and a half and, for once, I didn't even have to stay at the hospital! I would be home that very night.

There isn't a whole lot to tell about that one. I showed up. He looked over my chest and marked up my boobs again with a purple marker. He said that even without the fat grafting, they would come out great! Of course, that is always what the plastic surgeon is thinking about—appearance. Though, I will admit that I was happy he felt so confident in the outcome.

Present once again were the plastic surgeon and his two residents, the anesthesiologist and his two residents, and a handful of nurses. Nothing so fancy or dramatic as I've dealt with in the past. They put me out quick, and I don't even remember the operating room for this one. I woke up easily, though in a lot of pain. Of course, they had cut through the exact scar line that had just finished healing from September's job, making the incision sites extremely sore. For anyone that has scar tissue, especially thick scar tissue, you know that it usually hurts.

The incisions were sutured at the ends and heavily glued shut and all packaged quite tightly in what I dubbed the "torture bra." It is an ugly, front-clasping, mushroom-colored, one-size-too-small, squeezing-your-lungs-and-breasts as tight as possible contraption, so they don't move around during their initial healing. It was, hands down, the worst.

Luckily, though, my plastic surgeon's assistant came in and asked me—remembering our last conversation about medication—what I would like to take home for pain. I smiled and asked for Percocet. Last time was oxy, 10mg, with a recommendation to take one or two pills every four to six hours. This time, however, it was 5mg of oxy and 325mg of Tylenol. I felt like this was a safer and healthier choice.

Although I was in pain and wanted to rip that torture bra right off, I was thrilled—I was being discharged on the same day, and I was going home to recover in Christmas pajamas (provided by my best friend Sarah) where I would be able to recuperate in our winter-wonderland of a home so joyfully decorated by my husband and me.

I couldn't have been happier in that moment, considering everything.

Once home, there was a lot of lounging around. Or at least that's how the first couple of weeks went. I wore fluffy socks and a red-and-green flannel Victoria's Secret nightgown. It was loose and comfortable to wear; just what I needed at the time. Pumpkin spice and apple cinnamon candles were burning in almost every room, every day. There were twinkle lights on all the garlands, and the fancy tree stood in the living room, lit up around the clock.

One of my favorite treats after this surgery was delicious and delightful Christmas tree cookies from my local grocery store. They were just sugar cookies, but these had just a little something extra–something spicy–that made them perfect. Between Christmas and the pain meds, I felt pretty great for quite some time.

I noticed, though, as I weaned myself off the pain meds, that the scar tissue was tight and very painful to the touch when I stretched my arms out. Lifting even more than one plate at a time proved to be a difficult task. I was advised by the doctors to massage those areas to help loosen up the tissue. Doing this hurt, as you can imagine. And, even though the implant I held in my hand before the surgery felt squishy and jiggly, my breasts felt very firm and very unnatural.

Although the left side was the one that gave me the most trouble during the mastectomy recovery, the right-side scar tissue was now the most painful and thick. The scar tissue was like if my skin had been folded over three times, wrapped in Velcro, and then stapled shut. Tight, thick, and painful.

I realized that when I moved my arms or flexed, strange indentations appeared across my breasts. An odd rippling effect. Of course, I realized right away that those were the muscles that had been stretched over the implants. The fat grafting is what would have helped cover much of the flaws from being seen.

I had some regret, then; I won't lie. Seeing all the dimples and dents, ripples and odd shapes, I wished I'd had the grafting done. But honestly, those feelings lasted so briefly. The more and more I massaged my breasts to help them feel a little more natural, the more I grew accustomed to how they looked and accepted the choice I made. Primarily because here I was, approaching Christmas day without severe edema or bruising, or an abdominal binder, much less three more months of pain and recovery and a high risk of infection. Instead, I was approaching Christmas in cozy sweaters and comfortable jeans; fuzzy socks on; lit candles all around. I saw happiness rather than worry in my family's eyes.

My son Sabastion was fifteen years old at the time—he was very excited about the holiday, but most of all he was excited and relieved that I was in a good mood; in a good place. I felt the same way about him—I felt thankful that my husband could enjoy his favorite holiday (just like me!) without another hospital stay, or me being on drugs or waking in the middle of the night wracked with pain as the drugs wore off.

We decided we were determined to have the whole Christmas experience. This year, even though we had been chronically eating the delicious sugar cookies from the grocery store, we were going to bake from scratch the most amazing ginger cookies on earth. We baked ginger spice cookies with an orange clove icing. We perfected this recipe! We made it our own! In the end, I'm pretty sure we baked about five dozen.

They were perfection. I don't think I ever had a year of Christmas-cookie making where they all came out just so. I guess the true testament to their perfection is that I probably ate half of them on my own—or so I was often accused by my family. I even gave a tin to Dr. George during one of my sessions as Christmas approached.

The week of Christmas, we decided it was time for the real tree. Nick and I jumped in the car and drove to a local Home Depot, which in Tucson is one of the better places to buy a fresh tree. There were many kinds available, of course—the really cheap, giant, limp trees that barely hold your ornaments, an odd brownish green that you'd have to live in the desert to identify; then, there are the really fancy trees as I call them, with thick needles and strong, but sparse branches and that have an elegance to them. The needles on these are a bluish-green, like the skin of the agave plants that grow here.

I found the perfect tree. It stood right at six feet in height, perfectly round, with a straight-as-an-arrow top branch just for a star. When I found it, my husband was wandering around looking at other things. I couldn't lift the tree myself, still recovering as I was, so I simply set my hand on it and waited.

That is when it began–the Christmas tree sharks. They started circling, looking at my tree, asking me if I was just looking or if I was intent on purchasing. However, they hovered, waiting. Some walked away and came back. I didn't have my phone on me so I couldn't call my husband to tell him, so I stood there for quite some time just holding it. The sharks were obviously getting agitated.

Finally, Nick found me. He rescued me. He lifted up the tree and carried it to check out. He agreed that it was the picturesque tree of Christmas-card memories. We drove it home, covered it with as many colorful lights as it could carry, and got out all of the keepsake ornaments. We talked about each one as we put it on the tree–some came from trips we had taken, some brought back memories from when the children were young. Others still brought memories of Nick's mother. Many of them were from when Nick was a child. It was not just fun; it was intimate and precious. Even though it was not yet Christmas day, so far it had been the best Christmas I ever had.

As Christmas day grew closer, I grew restless, as I always do. I don't like to consider myself somebody who expects presents, but I have zero patience for surprises. So, when there is a present under the tree for me, it drives me absolutely crazy. I just have to know! It is not about the value or the quantity; it is the curiosity. I wonder how well that person knows me.

What did they get me that they thought would make me laugh, cry happy tears, or jump for joy? Because that is the kind of gift giver I am for everyone else. It is definitely not about the price; it is about sparking a twinkle in their eye.

Being raised extremely poor, as I was, and not even being able to recount any Christmases as a child—not for lack of memory, but because we simply didn't have them—I often made fantasy lists. These lists were often close to endless, made up of random things from throughout my life that I had always wanted. Some of the things could be pretty generic, others were commonplace, but a few were very precious and sought after—things I never anticipated actually having.

My husband, being the thoughtful, loving man that he is, wanted to make this Christmas extra special for me. It had been a hell of a year, I had been through a hell of a lot, and other than my engagement ring and wedding band I had never owned real diamonds.

On Christmas morning, one of those boxes had a pair of diamond earrings waiting for me inside. Being a girl, and now a woman, who had never thought much of herself and had never lived glamorously, I had always fantasized about owning something from Tiffany & Co.

On that same Christmas morning, in one of those coveted blue boxes, was a Return to Tiffany's bracelet—the exact one I always wanted.

There were many other beautiful gifts—sweaters, scarves, shoes—I felt spoiled, a feeling I was never accustomed to. I was overjoyed and had mixed emotions, caught between loving it all and wondering if I deserved it.

In the end, all that mattered to me that day was that everybody loved their gifts. Everyone laughed, ate, and enjoyed each other's company. It was the perfect day. To me, it felt like this was how Christmas was meant to be.

CHAPTER 13

THE FINAL CHALLENGE

It was a beautiful Christmas followed by a quiet and pleasant New Year. I was happy to be in January, as it is my birthday month. I was turning thirty-eight this year. My friend Danielle was coming to town, and all of my friends and what family I had were to gather together and have a big dinner. I looked forward to being able to laugh and talk without needing to worry about how I was feeling, for once.

It was a great birthday bash! I expected nothing but the presence of the people I care about and that is what I enjoyed the most. It felt nice to be able to dress up for once–to look alive, and attractive! Not to mention that it was an opportunity for people to interact with me in a positive, stress-free way for the first time in a long time.

The visit with Danielle was fabulous. The month of January was beautiful, and not terribly cold, although

I wished it had been. House projects continued, and I helped to the best of my ability. Family time was spent, and lots of laughs were had. I knew, though, that I was approaching something. The last piece of the BRCA puzzle. Come February 5th, they would remove the rest of my reproductive organs. This would completely clear my body of anything that could contribute to causing cancer, but also everything that made me, biologically, a woman.

I was nervous. I knew this meant menopause. I didn't know how I was going to react to it. What would it do to my body? Would I age faster? Would I lose my youth?

As the day approached, there was plenty of pre-screening, as usual, to ensure that I did not have any large cysts or tumors or other abnormalities prior to the surgery. I was hopeful, in some ways, as my surgeon, Dr. Grace, was an amazing woman and an amazing doctor. I had never come across a doctor who was so informative, detail oriented, and still so caring. She was genuinely and truly concerned about what was best for me in the short and the long run. She was pleasant to be around and spent quite a bit of time with me each visit. More than any other doctor, in my experience.

Perhaps most of all, she was the only surgeon who made me believe that the choice I had made was not only the right choice but the necessary choice. She was not just a gynecological oncologist; she was a prominent researcher in this field. She knew that the numbers were against me, as was time. She never made me feel that being less aggressive, playing a waiting game with monitoring, was preferable. She never made me feel like I was going to have unnecessary surgery.

She took extra caution, reading the full medical reports from my multiple surgeries since some had removed things from my abdomen. She was trying her best to guess what might be left, as previous surgical notes had left some ambiguity. After her review, she had a very concise and clear conversation with me. She thought it would be best to do a large incision–one, due to the scar tissue that riddled my abdomen, which made it difficult to find everything in the first place; and two, she was going to have to go on a hunt, searching for what leftover pieces may be inside me, like pieces of fallopian tube and other such pieces that could have been left there during previous surgeries.

I felt safe with her, but I was still scared. I'm not sure, at the time, what all of my fears were but I recall feeling sad that I was to be stripped of everything that made me different from a man–that made me a woman. I also remember feeling worried that my body was going to begin to wither away so early in my life and that I would become old, dried-up, and unattractive before my time. I know these seem like shallow fears, but being only thirty-eight-years old, and never truly, for the majority of my life, loving myself, this felt like it was going to be another blow.

In hindsight, though, I had no fucking idea.

Drying up, feeling old, not looking great–those were the least of the problems I would face.

$)($ $)($ $)($

February 5th rushed in. Here I was again, at the local university, for what would hopefully be my last surgery. I brought my bag, now expertly filled with the things I would need in the hospital. I did my paperwork and waited patiently to be called back. I was tired, as I was not allowed even coffee. Yawning, and in comfortable clothes, I heard my name called by a nurse. My husband and I, and my bag followed her back. We walked into a very familiar room, filled with sectioned-off curtained beds, with one designated for me.

I knew the routine all too well. I put my stuff down, took off my cozy clothes, and put on the gown. I knew shortly nurses would be coming in to hook up tubes, oxygen, and an IV of fluids. Beyond that, there would first be the appearance of the doctor, going over what we were going to do today just to make sure everyone was on the same page. This would be followed by a parade of other doctors and nurses who would be assisting, all introducing themselves and all explaining their role in the surgery. While the faces were different this time, the show ran the same way.

All this ended with the anesthesiologist giving me a dose of anti-anxiety drugs through my IV before I was wheeled off to the operating room. Once there, the anesthesiologist chatted with me a lot while the team prepped.

Dr. Grace walked up to me, just before I was put under. She touched my hand.

"Everything is going to be okay," she said.

I don't remember much after that.

I do remember waking up in pain. It was a lot. It was, in fact, the most pain I had ever experienced after any of my surgeries. It was a bit frightening and unexpected, considering how many abdominal surgeries I have had. I remember complaining, over and over again, to the nurses that it was unbearable. One of Dr. Grace's residents consulted with the nurses and me about giving me a small dose of pain medication. I didn't understand, then, why they hesitated–but I was glad to have it when it came.

Nick came back to the recovery area once he was allowed and realized that I was still in pain despite the medication they had given me. Eventually, I was moved to a room where I could recover. I was told that I could expect to be in the hospital for two nights, minimum. The pain was persistent, and yet the doses of pain meds were minimal and far between. I was asking for more "before it was time" according to the nurses, as it was barely helping.

Over the next twenty-four hours, the space between pain medication doses slowly grew without either of us really realizing it. I barely slept that night. By the middle of the next morning, it had been such a long time since my last dose of morphine that I found myself in so much pain, piercing horrible pain, that I couldn't control my crying or even sit still. I rocked in bed in a vain attempt to soothe my-self as I sobbed, my husband, looking on, worried and upset.

Prior to my surgery, I had made a plan with Dr. George for him to pay a visit again, just like during my mastectomy recovery. It happened that his visit took place during this period of distressing pain. As he has in the past, he sat down and patiently worked with me on "mindfulness," as he calls it. He asked me to envision a body of water. He had me walk into the water, in my mind–then sink down into the water and float. He asked me to describe everything I felt–from the tips of the hair on my head to the bottoms of my feet–as I floated away. At the same time, he used the aromatherapy I brought along with me to the hospital–I mixed it myself since I was inspired by his use of it during previous surgeries and sessions. He sprayed it every so often. The smell reminded me of the ocean.

He stayed a long time. Sometimes he just watched me drift off a little bit, as exhausted as I was. He stayed with me until I knew, and he knew, that I was going to be okay. I got the sense that he didn't want to leave me alone.

That same morning Russ was planning to visit to see how I was doing. It happened that he interrupted Dr. George and me, and at that point, Dr. George decided he would leave, likely feeling reassured that I would have someone close to me at my side.

Just as Russ's visit interrupted Dr. George and me, Russ's visit was now interrupted by another attack of terrible pain. It was at that point that it occurred to all of us that something was going on. Why wasn't I receiving the kind of pain management I had received after every other surgery? Why was I being made to suffer? Now at the point of being angry, my husband went to find out.

One of the nurses came back in with him. She seemed surprised and concerned to see me in so much pain. She said she would page the resident doctor to find out if I could receive pain medication. In the meantime, she administered the one pain medication, as I found out then, I was allowed to have. That was Toradol, which is basically liquid ibuprofen.

Eventually, word came that the doctor had okayed oxycodone pills and that the pharmacy was working on it. Meanwhile, I was still rocking myself in an attempt to self-soothe while I moaned in agony. My husband and Russ, no longer able to just sit and watch me suffer, both stormed down to the internal pharmacy–buried in a distant basement hallway–to push the pharmacist to fill it quickly. I guess they made a compelling case, as the pharmacist, likely against protocol, filled it immediately.

While much slower than morphine, I finally got some relief from the pain.

It was a little bit later that second day that we found out what was behind this disaster of a situation. The resident doctor showed up doing her rounds, and my husband and I both asked her why I had been denied pain medication earlier, and what the intent was behind switching to pills. This was so unlike other recoveries–hell, when I had my

ovary rupture the previous March I got a self-serve morphine button!

The doctor explained her reasoning—she said that she
had read my file and noted that, after my mastectomy, I
told the doctor I felt the oxycodone pills had become
addictive and that I had suffered from withdrawal
symptoms. Because of this, she felt it was best to get me
off morphine as quickly as possible and minimize the
amount of pain meds I received. I was livid and devastated. Because I had been honest and proactive, with an
interest in my own health, I had now been labeled. I was
an addict in their eyes.

Because of this, and the conclusions the doctor had
jumped to, I had been tortured. Having your morphine
pulled less than a day after extreme abdominal surgery
was inhumane. Thankfully, Dr. Grace agreed. She made
her rounds later that afternoon, and I spoke up to her
about the pain medication issue. She seemed baffled. She
explained to me, with her resident standing behind her
shoulder looking sheepish, why I was in so much pain. Not
only was the incision large, but she had to cut away huge
amounts of intestinal and abdominal scar tissue and explore my entire abdomen, looking for the missing parts
and pieces.

Shaking her head, she said that while she didn't want
to overdo the pain medication because of my previous
bowel obstruction—as pain medication slows bowel movement—she also didn't see any reason that I needed to be

in this much pain. Overruling her resident, she ordered regular dosing of morphine for the remainder of my stay. Thank God for Dr. Grace.

ꭓ ꭓ ꭓ

The rest of my relatively short hospital stay (just a few days long) was fairly pleasant, as they go. Russ and Roxanne came back to visit me together. They stayed a while, as they tend to do, talking about what was next for me medically and what to expect. Roxanne helped me get comfortable in my own pajamas that I had brought along to the hospital. We enjoyed one another's company until my next medication dose. They left as I drifted off.

It wasn't much longer beyond that before I was released, discharged from the hospital, and back home. It was an uncomfortable recovery at home as well, but it wasn't just the incision site and other related surgical pain.

My body was doing things, things I didn't expect. I was exhausted. I couldn't get out of bed in the morning. I found myself taking naps during the day—even as a very nap adverse person! I found myself with an onset of extreme hot flashes—sweat dripping, overwhelming hot flashes. With those hot flashes came mood swings—tears for no reason, over tiny petty things. Sometimes I was starving, and other times I wouldn't be interested in food at all. I was all over the board, but at the time I was trying to deal.

About a week after surgery my husband took me out on a Friday morning, while still on medical leave to help me recover, to get some fresh air, walk around, window shop—mainly, to try and help cheer me up and take my mind off of things. While we were out, one of my newfound mood swings hit. We were at HomeGoods, one of our favorite places to browse for housewares, when it slammed into me full force. I tried to keep it at bay, inside, but Nick noticed that something was wrong. We left, and headed on to another store, talking in the car on the way there.

Unable to simply deal anymore, I started to describe all of the things I had been going through lately. The feelings I had let go unspoken. Once I started to talk, it was like the floodgates opened. I cried as I told him that it had become unbearable. Scariest of all, to us both, I revealed to him that along with my mood swings I was being tormented by my own desires to hurt myself. To end my life, somehow.

We decided, then, that help was needed. Now.

I got on the phone to the Cancer Center and asked to speak with Dr. Grace's nurse. That was the usual line of communication with the doctor's there—you spoke with their nurse, who acted as the messenger, the middleman. Doctors didn't talk on the phone.

I explained to her nurse, easily one of the sweetest people I'd dealt with during this experience, what I had been experiencing, where I was today, and why I thought

I needed help. She seemed genuinely worried and said she would speak with Dr. Grace right away.

Immediately after hanging up, I called Dr. George as well. We had talked about some of this during a session just the afternoon prior, so he was fairly up-to-speed, but I explained how Nick and I had realized I needed more immediate help. I couldn't wait until my scheduled follow-up with Dr. Grace. Dr. George said he would call and ask to speak with Dr. Grace himself.

It couldn't have been much more than an hour later, just as we pulled up to T.J. Maxx, that my phone rang. It was the number of the cancer center, so I fully expected to hear the nurse on the line with some advice or plan. However, when I said "Hello," I was surprised to find Dr. Grace on the other end of the line.

"I have been in this field for many years, now, and this is the first time in my career that a psychiatrist has called me with concerns about our mutual patient," she said. This, she went on to explain, is why she made the call and made it with such haste.

We spoke for some time about what I had been experiencing since the surgery. Dr. Grace, being the person that she is, was genuinely sympathetic and sorry that I was going through this. And, at the same time, she was very direct about her solution.

"My goal was to avoid putting you on hormones so soon after surgery. The risk of blood clots is high after surgery, and it is high on hormones, so the risk is exponentially higher together. However, I believe it is a risk we must take to help you avoid any risk of harming yourself. That isn't a risk I am willing to take."

In the end, the decision was to start me on a regimen of 1mg of hormone replacement medication right away. Then, at our follow-up, if all was well she would increase the dose to 2mg. It turns out, they were the key at the time. Once I started taking them, I began to feel better–less fatigue-prone, fewer mood swings, less frequent and intense hot flashes. I was able to pull myself together. I even got myself to start walking the two-mile route at the river path. My mind became set on getting back to the zoo–back to my elephants–back to life. In the same light, I became more active around the house again. I got back to cleaning, walking the dogs, pushing my limits daily, slowly increasing my stamina. I made contact with the zoo, giving them a return date so they could expect me and also to give myself a hard date by which I wanted to be back in shape enough to work there. It was my way of motivating myself.

Back when I was volunteering pre-surgeries, I had over time increased my work schedule to work three days per week. I remembered that Wednesday was typically the day they were light on volunteers, so I picked a Wednesday three months out, on May 9th.

I told them that I would give them one day a week of my time to start to see how I did and work my way back up from there. At this point I was pushing myself harder, going to the gym as frequently as I could muster, and just working through daily life.

)( )( )(

It was creeping up on May. I found myself in the backyard doing some gardening and yard work. I loved being outside, and it wasn't quite summertime hot yet. As I trimmed all of our flowering bushes, raked and swept, I felt like I was ready. While working in the backyard was difficult, I won't lie, I felt like if I could do this, I could definitely tough out being back at the zoo. It might be hard in the beginning but being around the keepers and those precious elephants would make it all feel worth it.

May approached quickly, and then it was May 9th. I was nervous and excited. The nervousness was more worry than anything–that I would not be able to keep up, or that I would forget things, or not know how to answer questions about all the absences I had. That said, I was returning, and that was the biggest thing to me. I had done it–I lived–and I was going back!

Driving to the zoo that early morning I felt alive. Fully geared up, right down to the work boots, with my Luna bar and yogurt in my bag, having eaten my morning banana and had my morning cup of coffee, armed with a giant container of ice water–nothing was missing–I was ready to go.

I sat in on the early zoo meeting as usual. I exchanged smiles with the keepers that I knew as they walked in. Afterward, we all headed back for the elephant area. Things were a little different than what I remembered a usual morning start being like. We started in the yard–that was the same–but a few keepers were missing. From what I heard, they were in the barn. The rest of us kept working. Once we cleared the yard, all seven acres, this other volunteer and I (we had never met before) were in the hay barn cleaning up. We were doing more than usual in the hay barn. By this time, usually, we would have shifted to the paddocks.

Mara, one of the younger keepers, came out and told us that there was a delay. We were told to keep working in the hay barn until further notice, that the other elephants were being shifted out to the yard, but that Punga was not. He was being monitored by staff and the vet.

She didn't say much, except that he was having stomach issues. She walked back into the elephant barn. I felt a sense of worry like I wasn't hearing the whole story.

Some time went by. I'm not sure how long. We were essentially done with what we could do and found ourselves waiting. Then, a commotion arose. More staff, running into the elephant barn. I knew. Nobody had told me anything yet, but I knew. I felt myself denying it. I stood there, without any mood or expression on my face, waiting. I did not want it to be true. I couldn't swallow; my chest got tight.

Mara walked back out, slowly, toward us. She had no expression on her face. She said that we were being sent home for the day. She said she appreciated our help, and that she was sorry.

"What happened?" I asked.

"Punga died."

She cried. As soon as she said it, she couldn't hold back her tears. The new volunteer, standing with us, reached out and hugged her.

I stared at her. I said, "I'm so sorry," as I tried to hold back my own tears.

She turned around and began to walk away then stopped and turned back at us and said, "I would appreciate it if you would keep this confidential until we release it to the press. There needs to be some time to mourn and an understanding of what happened."

We both shook our heads, agreeing.

I walked to my car. It felt like everything around me was completely silent. Like I was in shock. My brain kept trying to say that it just wasn't true. I got in my car, started it, and sat for a few minutes. Then, I cried. Hysterically. Just cried. I wanted so badly to go in there and see him, but I knew I couldn't. I knew I'd never see him again. I was overwhelmed with an awful feeling of loss.

I called Nick. I knew he wouldn't tell anybody. I cried to him on the phone, and then I tried to pull myself together.

I drove home.

)( )( )(

A whole week passed. It was Wednesday again. Zoo day. I felt reluctant, still sad and distraught. I didn't know how I would go about what was supposed to be a normal day when nothing about it felt normal. Yet, I returned and tried to work through.

We cleared the yard, and things went as scheduled. We moved to the inside portion. They were still holding an elephant back from the yard at that point, which was unusual. It was Mabu, the father, who had returned while I was out during surgical leave. Mabu had fathered all of the children with Semba. He was being held because he was having stomach problems.

This is the first time I had ever laid eyes on Mabu. He was enormous, a sight to be seen. He was something akin to a portrait, he was so perfect—a picturesque beast straight from the African wilds. I couldn't appreciate his beauty fully, though, as I felt sick to my stomach in that instant. I was worried—was something going to happen to him too? I guess it was written all over my face.

Cassie said, "We're so sorry your first day back was such a bad day. It was a bad day for us all." Looking back toward the massive elephant in the room, she said, "We're just being cautious with Mabu."

I was sent home early that day. It was a tough day physically and emotionally. I hadn't experienced a full day, or really even close to one yet. Not since my return. But I recognized that day that it was tough to keep up with the volunteer duties, and the expectation for speed that the tasks required. I was hurting, and it showed.

)(   )(   )(

I returned the following Wednesday, once again. It was a full day that time. No complications with the elephants. Mabu was just fine. All was back to normal. Except for me. I struggled. I had spent the entire week between volunteer days recovering but never really did. The work was hard, and it seemed to only pile onto the fatigue and soreness I felt. After pushing through as best as I could, I went home. I thought about it long and hard. I decided to tell Cassie that I needed some more time before I could return. That I was struggling and perhaps was not ready–that maybe, I had returned too soon.

She was kind and understanding, saying, "I hope to hear back from you sometime later this summer."

I won't make anyone wait–she didn't hear from me. At least, not about volunteering again.

I was finding myself in a whole new reality. I learned new things about my body, post-surgeries, almost every day. New quirks, new aches, new limitations. It was quickly clear to me that I had returned too soon. I hadn't given myself time to understand myself, in my drive to become an apprentice and eventually an elephant keeper. My new self.

CHAPTER 14

FACING THE
ELEPHANTS

At first I felt like I had failed, but looking back, how could I possibly blame myself?

Not only had my body been wracked to the edge of death once again, and put through the surgical wringer, but here I was at age thirty-eight entering early onset menopause. I was taking fists-full of medication that I had never even heard of before in an attempt to wrangle the crazy symptoms my sudden lack of hormones left me with. Even with that, some of them were impossible to abate–like the earth shaking hot flashes I would get. Sweat-inducing hot flashes that made me want to rip off all of my clothes no matter where I was! How could I have expected myself to handle that at the zoo, during the summer?

As the months dragged on without any sign of a miraculous physical recovery, I was forced to consider the possibility that my body may have a new normal. Would I, despite my "go get 'em" attitude and powerful perseverance, simply never be up for such a physically demanding job again?

As I continued to struggle with my physical being, my mental being also began to raise its own set of questions. Losing Punga, a member of the elephant family, had destroyed me inside and out (I am crying as I write this, just thinking about him) to the extent that I would never have expected. I love all animals, and can't stand to see any one animal suffer, but elephants are, as you now know, different for me. When he died, a piece of my heart was excised from my body. Ripped out, Indiana Jones style.

How would I handle it not if, but when, another elephant at the zoo fell ill? Could I take it, years later, when I would be just that much more connected to them, in the event that Semba passed? Could I really watch Nandi grieve her mother's passing without falling to pieces myself?

These thoughts plagued me for months, day in and day out. It was a vicious battle between my love for the elephants, my tendency to expect perfection of myself, and reality.

XXX

It was a hot summer night, mid-July, a year after from my bowel obstruction surgery. I had a dream that night, and it changed me.

A hot, dry breeze blows across the African savannah.

I sit in the middle of the open grassland, a line of trees about 500 yards in front of me.

Out from the trees wanders a small family of elephants.

A gigantic bull, almost prehistoric in size, and rugged.

An older-looking female, an air of wisdom and sadness, and strength too, about her.

A mother, protective of her baby. Still youthful.

A pair of boys, playful, not quite bulls yet.

Lastly, that baby. Running around between the legs of the rest like a typical toddler.

My heart flutters. As the small family of elephants meanders closer, I know it is my family of elephants. After some time, they draw near to me. They trumpet as if to greet me.

I desire nothing else but to run toward them, to hug them and pet their rough, granite-like sides. I can't, though. My legs won't work beneath my body. I realize, then that I am paralyzed. I can look around but do nothing about it.

I scream a voiceless scream and wished I could pound the hot, dry dirt. I cry tears that evaporate off my cheeks in the hot African sun. I sit, facing the elephants, powerless.

Nandi walks forward with a gentle nudge from Semba. The rest stay behind. When she stands just inches from me, her youthful face bright with curiosity and innocence, her tiny trunk reaches out and wraps around my hand.

With glee, I find I can now stand, if only slowly at first. I start to stumble my way toward the elephants when Nandi gives me a gentle yank in the other direction. Then she leads me at first hesitantly, toward the edge of the precipice of the cliff behind me.

Standing near the edge, she lets go of my hand and playfully waves her trunk at the horizon. I look out and gasp at what I see.

Stretched before me is an endless grassland. It is dotted with shapes, as far as the eye can see. Herds of elephants. Thousands, maybe more!

I look down at Nandi only to realize she is looking up at me. She reaches out with her trunk and gently touches my cheek before turning around and playfully bounding back to her family. She rejoins the line, bleating out a young elephant call.

It strikes me, then. I am compelled. I clamber down the precipice and begin my trek into the land of elephants laid out before me.

I woke, sweat-drenched, with a whole new perspective.

)( )( )(

I was never destined to be an elephant keeper. I now knew that. My journey to the zoo was not about that. Instead, I realized what elephants had really been to me my whole life; whether in dreams or in the real world, elephants were my guides.

I know now that the purpose of my time volunteering at the zoo was not about my career or what I would do next to make a living. It was about being knocked off track after the events of 2014. It was about needing a steady guiding hand through all the surgeries yet to come. I was lost, and as they did in my dream, elephants there showed me the way.

As the realizations unfolded on me, in that moment, I understood what my purpose was. I had to tell my story.

I had to tell it for me, to help rid myself of the scars on my mind and body created by the outside world.

I had to tell it for other women facing medical hardships, murky decisions, and devastating outcomes as they worked to stay alive despite the odds.

I had to tell it for the elephants, these creatures so much more than just animals. Spiritual icons, disregarded so often by humankind, threatened with extinction.

This book is my purpose, manifested.

It is also just the start. Something significant must come of all the hardship I've faced. I know those hardships are the vehicle by which I am able to extend my ability to help myself, to help other women, and to help elephants.

I will tell my story anywhere I can.

I will start a women's health support group in my town.

I will put my time, money, and voice toward causes that help protect elephants all over the world.

With elephants at my side, I am unstoppable.

EXPEDITION TANZANIA

W hile volunteering for the zoo I had the unique opportunity to be invited to attend a talk on elephant conservation by one of the leading advocates in the field, Tim Davenport. I went out of my love for the elephants, and out of curiosity–I wanted to hear what someone who worked amongst elephants, at home and abroad, had to say.

What I came away with, though, was much more profound.

Tim's talk centered on the plight of African elephants, at risk more than ever, and how he and the Wildlife Conservation Society's (WCS) Tanzania Project were working to preserve elephant populations.

Tim is obviously a brilliant man–that was clear to me as I listened to him. He is tall and lanky and wears a newsy hat. He speaks with a British accent and is a graduate of Leeds. He told a story about a kid who came to his camp in Tanzania where he was working with the elephants. He called him a kid, but he was obviously just an inexperienced young man. He spoke about how they had to go somewhere and "the kid" got into the Jeep as an elephant came out of the bush. It was a feisty elephant, evident from the posturing and sounds it was making.

He recounted that the Jeep wouldn't start. The kid started to panic. Tim gave him guidance on what to do and not do. However, the elephant was a big bull, and it approached them and rocked the Jeep. The next day Tim said he had to brief the other compatriots that they'd be one person short for the rest of the trip. He laughed at the memory.

He went into great detail about the people of Tanzania who worked with the protected elephants. He held them in high respect—the men there had essentially grown up beside these elephants.

He said he didn't understand why a segment of people hated zoos. He spoke about the feeling people have of hatred for the lack of freedom of zoo animals, but from his perspective, zoos not only protect threatened species, but they donate large amounts of time and money to conservation. Not only that, but they give the average person an opportunity to enjoy seeing a rare animal while educating them to their plight. Even if only a small percentage of visitors came away impacted, driven to do something about the problem, the world could change.

Audience members at his talk kept raising their hands, asking how they could help. Every time his answer was, "Write a check." He kept reiterating that as long as there is poaching and development in and around the habitat of African elephants, there would be a strong need for funding to support conservation programs like the Tanzania project.

I left that night admiring Tim, and with a new appreciation for the plight of elephants.

Below is an excerpt from the WCS Tanzania project website:[1]

"Tanzania harbours one of Africa's most significant remaining elephant populations, the only larger population being found in Botswana. In 1976, numbers in Tanzania stood at 316,000, but major declines in the late 1980s and especially since 2009, driven by an upsurge in the illegal trade in ivory, have decimated the population which today stands at roughly 45,000.

Historically, many of the countries significant elephant areas formed part of an elephant meta-population, with substantial dispersal between areas such as the Selous and northern Mozambique and Rua-ha-Katavi and the north. Substantial habitat still ex-

---

1 "TANZANIA PROGRAM." Tanzania Program, ©WCSTANZANIA 2016, tanzania.wcs.org/Species/Elephant.aspx.

ists in many areas, but improved understanding is needed to verify to what extent historical corridors remain viable and in use.

Conservation of Tanzania's elephants is therefore focused on rapidly improving understanding related to elephant ranging so that improved protection can be promoted in both core areas as well as interlinking corridors. Where elephants come into contact with people, the mitigation of human-elephant conflict where possible is also an essential approach."

Yes, even in this day, ivory poaching is not just commonplace but, in fact, has exploded due to a spike in demand for ivory. I went on to learn, too, that the plight is not much different for Asian elephants. Another excerpt, this time from the World Wildlife Federation.[2]

Habitat loss and conflict with communities

"In the face of rapidly growing human populations, the Asian elephants' habitat is shrinking fast and wild elephant populations are mostly small, isolated, and unable to mingle as ancient migratory routes are cut off by human settlements.

---

2 "Asian Elephants–Threats." WWF, © WWF-International, wwf.panda. org/knowledge_hub/endangered_species/elephants/asian_elephants/ asianeleph_threats/.

Large development projects (such as dams, roads, mines and industrial complexes), plantations, and spreading human settlements have fragmented what was once contiguous elephant habitat into small fragments.

Incidents of elephants raiding crops and villages are on the rise. This causes losses to human property and, sometimes, human lives. Retaliation by villagers often results in killings of these elephants. Experts already consider such confrontations to be the leading cause of elephant deaths in Asia.

In some countries, the government provides compensation for crop damage or deaths caused by elephants, but there is still often strong political pressure on wildlife authorities to eliminate elephants near populated regions. As human populations increase, human-elephant conflicts are likely to increase.

Illegal hunting and trade
In Asian elephants, only males carry tusks and therefore poaching is aimed exclusively at males. Selective removal of tuskers for their ivory may lead to an increase in the proportion of tuskless males in the population.

Poaching of Asian elephants for ivory remains a threat in some countries. However, most illegal ivory currently comes from African sources, rather than from Asian elephants.

Elephants are also taken from the wild for the live elephant trade – primarily going to Thailand for the tourism industry.

India, Vietnam, and Myanmar have banned capture in order to conserve their wild herds, but in Myanmar, elephants are still caught each year for the timber industry or the illegal wildlife trade.

Unfortunately, crude capture methods have led to a high mortality level. Efforts are being made not only to improve methods but also to encourage captive breeding rather than taking from the wild."

Preservation of elephants is the strongest of my many passions. As you read, they have brought comfort and safety, inspiration and strength, to me throughout a very difficult life.

If you have discovered a passion for elephants too, don't let it end at collecting stuffed animals and wearing T-shirts. Don't just collect knick-knacks. See elephants for more than the trendy design they may be these days. In the great words of Tim Davenport, "Write a check."

ABOUT THE AUTHOR

Rebecca Black has a dark past. She has lived many lives, from working for the Department of Child Welfare to teaching as an adjunct professor. She is a survivor and BRCA1 previvor. She has also died—three times. In the midst of it all, she has found a physical connection and a spiritual purpose with a family of elephants.

Rebecca was born in Michigan but grew up in Tucson, Arizona, where she lives today with her husband, two sons, and two dogs. She loves art—especially Gustav Klimt. She adores music—Tori Amos, Otis Redding, and Radiohead. She is an eclectic, fierce woman.

Facing the Elephants is her debut memoir.

authorrebeccablack.com

Instagram @r.black8890